In a Whisper

A Trick Horse Training Manual

By Suzanne Fargher

Featuring 'Fern'

Photos & Illustrations by Kris & Suzanne Fargher

Suzanne Fargher has been a keen Horse-woman for approximately 20 years.

With her passion for natural Horseman-ship, training and equine communication, she demonstrates with the help of her horsey friend Fern how everyone can learn to 'whisper', practising the art of Circensic dressage.

She lives in the Isle of Man with her husband Kris and her pretty palomino mare Fern.

In a Whisper

A Trick Horse Training Manual

By Suzanne Fargher & Fern

Photographs & Illustrations by Kristen & Suzanne Fargher

Published in Great Britain 2010

Suzanne Fargher

The Studio, No 3, Barrule House

126 Bucks Road, Douglas

Isle of Man IM1 3AH

Text & Images Copyright © Suzanne Fargher 2010

British Library Cataloguing-in-Publication Data.

A catalogue record for this book is available from the British Library

All rights reserved. No part of the book, text, photographs or illustrations, may be reproduced or transmitted in any form or by any means by print, photo print, Micro-film, microfiche, photocopier, or in any way known or as yet unknown or stored in a retrieval system, without prior written permission from the author Suzanne Fargher.

Disclaimer of Liability:

The author and publisher shall have neither liability nor responsibility to any person or entity with respect to any loss, damage or injury caused or alleged to be caused directly or indirectly by the information contained in this book. While the book is as accurate as the author can make it, there may be errors, omissions and inaccuracies.

Dedication

Thank-you to my dear long suffering, dedicated & patient Husband Kris for his constant help and encouragement, to my fantastic parents for their long and faithful years of support during my pony mad childhood! To the beautiful star of this book, Fern who has been such an amazing inspiration, to Kylie O'Brien & Karen Mackison for their help with the book, and in loving memory of Blue, Pip, Willow, Cashew & Cassie, who all taught me so much!

Contents

Words of Caution-Safety First 8
Introduction 10
The Author and Her Beautiful Assistant 15
Tools & Props 16
Chapter 1: Back to Basics 17
Understand Your Equine Friend! 18
Can Any Horse Learn Tricks? 26
Analyse & Listen to Your Horse 28
Remember to Say Sorry! 33
Golden Rules to Successful Trick Training 34
Trick or Treat 39
Challenge Your Imagination 42
Chapter 2: Laying Good Foundations 42
Yielding to Pressure 44
Introducing Clicker Training 46
Stand Still & Correct 47
Back Up 49
Circle Away 49
The Side Pass 52
Chapter 3: First Steps 54
Say Cheese!!! The Perfect Smile 55
Give Us a Big Sloppy Kiss! 57
How About a Hug Then? 58
Oh so Shy! 60
Yes & No 61
Give Us a Push! 63
Left & Right Please! 64
Let's Shake On It! 66
What's 1 + 1 =? 67

The Stretch!	68
End of Trail Pose	70
Chapter 4: Introducing Props	72
Hold a Target Object	73
Toot Your Own Horn!	74
Can I Take Your Hat Ma'am?	76
Hitting the Bottle!	77
Had a Drink Have We?	79
The Flag Wave	81
Little Pick-Pocket	83
Play Ball!	85
Chapter 5: Clever Clogs	86
The Bow 'Obeisance'	88
Kneeling or 'Arabian Prayers'	94
Lie Down	96
Take a Seat	101
Sit Up please!	104
Curtsy or Circus Bow	108
Queen's Curtsy	111
Chapter 6: Pedestal Work	114
Introducing the Box	115
Pirouette on the Box	121
Curtsy Bow on the Box	122
Chapter 7: Fancy Footwork! The Finale	123
Spanish Walk	125
The Rear & Collected Variations	130
The Buck Jump	136
Summary	140
Appendix 1: How to Make Your Own Rope Halter	142

7

Words of Caution-Safety First

All elements of riding, training & handling horses carry a certain level of risk. It is up to you, as the responsible handler, to ensure you exercise the appropriate caution and patience in everything you do to protect yourself, and your horse, and to avoid dangerous situations from developing.

Realistically and honestly assess your own abilities before you attempt any of these tricks on your own; you owe this to yourself and your horse. It is wise to work with an experienced trainer if you do not have the skills or confidence necessary to safely try any of these tricks by yourself. A responsible and experienced adult should always supervise young children.

Throughout training you must consistently demand complete respect, manners and discipline from your horse. Most horses enjoy this training so much they get carried away and forget they are playing with a human rather than another horse, resulting in colourful bruises or worse. In return you must always treat the horse with the same manners and respect that you would expect to receive.

When teaching your horse tricks, always document learned behaviours and any cues your horse becomes familiar with. Keep this information safe with your horse's records. This is important for practical reasons. If your horse is handled by others or ever sold, these notes will ensure that the horse is safely handled and it is not misunderstood. Otherwise it could be labelled a problem animal, due to people accidentally cueing trick behaviour without realising it. Consider it your trick horse owner's manual.

Whilst trick training is fun and an interesting way of enjoying your horse's company, please think long and hard if you really want your horse to learn each trick. If he does, are you confident that you can control it once the behaviour is established? For example it would not be wise to teach a child's pony to rear for obvious reasons. You may be comfortable with it, but future owners are unlikely to be prepared or experienced enough to manage the behaviour.

Lastly, always remember to use appropriate safety gear for you and your horse to prevent injury. Trick training should be fun. Practice safely and sensibly and you will both have years of enjoyment learning, teaching and performing your new talents. Happy Training!

9

Introduction

Trick training, otherwise known as Circensic Dressage, is a fascinating pursuit. It is not only highly entertaining, fun and rewarding, but also strengthens the relationship between horse and handler. It builds an additional avenue of natural communication and understanding within the partnership. Your horse learns to pay attention to you, becomes more responsive and respectful, and actually learns how to read you, becoming smarter, and more confident as he progresses in his training.

Most owners would love to teach their four-legged friend a trick or a movement or two. Sadly there can be a lack of knowledge, time, patience or clear understanding about how horses learn. What should be a fun experience for horse and trainer, turns to confusion, frustration, miscommunication, training and behaviour problems, and finally giving up.

On embarking on this training journey myself, I looked for books and videos on the subject. To my surprise, there were very few to be found. Most trick trainers and performers protect their training secrets in order to wow the crowds and preserve the magic of their craft. Like a secret society or the 'magic circle', many trainers take their knowledge to the grave rather than share their valuable wisdom with others. It is a great shame when such learning dies with its owner, and I believe this is why many of the great training secrets have been lost and long forgotten. So I have put together this guide from my own diary of experiences and training notes whilst bringing up my young palomino mare Fern. Hopefully I can share something extraordinary with you and perhaps inspire you to give it a try yourself.

So, why bother to teach tricks at all? Tricks are fun and fulfilling to teach, but can also be used to establish a natural vocabulary and understanding between horse and handler that can be applied in almost any given situation. It is also a marvellous way of relaxing your horse and encouraging confidence in young or nervous animals. As you progress, you will begin to understand how your horse learns and this, in turn, allows you to work together more effectively and be more creative with your tricks and general training. It will strengthen your bond and trust in each other. It will also suddenly dawn on you what the famous horse whisperers are all about, and that it is not just a gift for the selected few. Anybody can learn these skills.

'Whispering' is purely a very deep, almost spiritual understanding of how the horse ticks. This accomplishes an extraordinary level of communication between horse and human. The few who achieve it, can work in true harmony, attaining a deep bond with their horses. You will be able to think how horses think. You will be able to read them and manipulate their natural behaviour to perform how you wish, willingly and voluntarily, without opposition or objection. Suddenly your horse will stop seeing you as a predator. He will learn to respect you as a partner and herd leader, as someone to follow and trust, with whom they want to spend quality time. Your horse will grow in intelligence and character. He will actually crave the stimulation of learning and attention that's bestowed on him, turning his training into a game for praise and reward.

Horses can begin trick training at any age. However like children, every horse learns at their own speed, so keep at it. It is important to remember that if the horse is having trouble learning, then the problem lies with the teacher. Never blame the horse! It is up to us to communicate in horse language and not for the horse to try and understand ours! So if this happens, look at your own body language and methods, and ensure that you are asking for something correctly. When communicating you must be correct in your actions and clear and consistent so your horse will be able to follow and understand. Many problems arise from us just not being clear with our instructions thus causing our poor four-legged friends much angst and confusion. Successful training of horses depends as much on our behaviour and demeanour as it does on our equine friends.

Imagine if you will, a gentleman who only speaks ancient Greek, he is trying to talk you through complicated algebraic equations. Now more than 99.9999 % of us would struggle to understand what he was saying let alone understand the point of his lesson. Congratulations! You are now seeing things from your horse's perspective; most folk are trying to communicate extremely complicated lessons to another creature in a language it does not understand expecting to get amazing results.

Unfortunately they then get completely frustrated and wonder what on earth is wrong when the 'stupid' horse doesn't immediately do what has been asked. This is why we must speak the horse's language. If we want them to learn for us then we must first make the effort to learn to communicate effectively with them.

Trick training is often criticised as a waste of time, demeaning to the horse and an activity only suitable for the circus ring and amusement of others. These comments are often made by those who do not appreciate the knowledge, trust and commitment required to achieve this level of training. Much is gained both by the human and horse and the same training can then be applied to everyday life and schooling. This book is not intended to ridicule or demean the horse in anyway, but hopefully proves the horse is a highly intelligent creature capable of thought and reasoning who loves to learn and play!

12

Unfortunately there are many who horrifically abuse and beat innocent animals to perform at will for entertainment purposes. Behaviour like this is inexcusable. This is one of the many reasons why I wish to demonstrate that we can work together with these beautiful creatures, working in harmony and with respect, learning from each other, enjoying each other's company, having fun practising and testing our communication through these light hearted games and tricks. When the horse enjoys and looks forward to learning and performing, you will have a happy contented animal who will always try his best for you!

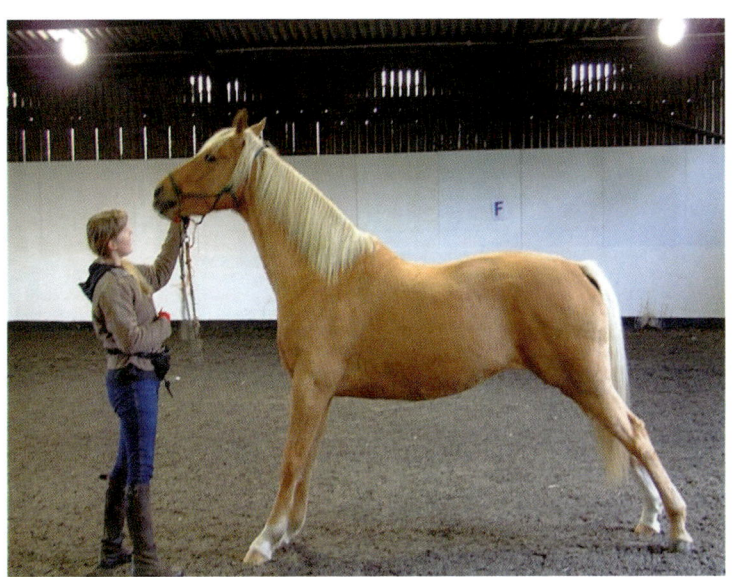

Once a horse has been taught these methods of learning they can be put to practical use. For instance, a horse can be taught to bow or lie down to assist those with restricted mobility to mount easily. A horse scared to cross a bridge or enter a trailer can be taught to happily and confidently face these fears through the same approach.

Trick training also demonstrates the amazing feats that can be achieved once the human to horse communication barriers have been broken down. This surely confirms that communication, and what we can learn from it, enlightens every other aspect of our relationship with the horse and how we approach every day training and handling.

This book will explain how your horse ticks, give you tips on the secrets of communication, some basic foundation handling games to help you practice your skills and establish your dominance as leader of the herd. This is the ultimate test of your training skills, leading you through a step-by-step learning curve to whispering through the fascinating and fun world of trick training.

Remember, you may consider your faithful four-legged friend a star already, but if you persevere you will soon be the proud partner of a Super Star!

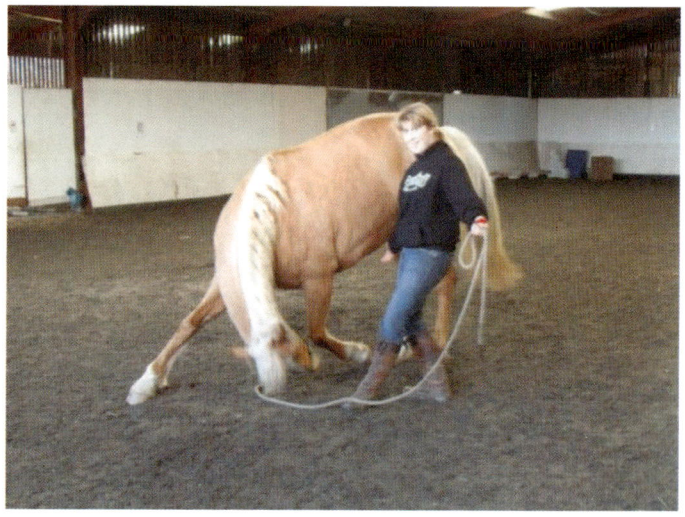

The Author and Her Beautiful Assistant

Self taught Trick & Natural Horsemanship trainer Suzanne Fargher has been a horse owner for more than 20 years. In this time she has made it her goal to work with her horses, using an in-depth knowledge of horse psychology, love, patience and understanding to create a unique and enviable partnership with her animals. The resulting level of communication is undeniably the stuff of horse whispering legends and truly can be taught to anybody willing to focus on learning the methods and who accept that they have more to learn than their horse!

'Fern' or 'Fernoodle' to her friends!

Introducing 'Fern', a gorgeous charismatic three quarters Thoroughbred x Welsh Cob. Foaled June 30th 2001, in the town of Rogate, Petersfield, Hants, Southern England. She was registered in the British Palomino Society as 'Champagne Bubbles'. She is the daughter of Donna's Red out of Tinker, and grand-daughter of Clan Time & Lightening Gem. Purchased as a yearling in 2002 by Suzanne Fargher she moved to the Isle of Man where she is now just starting a promising career in Circensic dressage and display work!

Fern loves games, being the centre of attention, carrots, the Farrier's bottom and chasing dogs! She dislikes, dentists, winter days and early mornings.

Tools & Props

16

For most of the tricks and movements within this book you will need some basic tools and equipment to get you started, most of which you will probably have already. You will also need to obtain and utilise the appropriate safety equipment for yourself and your horse. Each section will advise exactly what equipment is needed for each trick and how to use it. Remember to always use the minimum equipment needed to get your horse to perform.

Basic equipment needed for training:-
- Rope Head collar, Type made from Marine ¼" Double Braided Nylon
- Normal Lead rope
- 12 to 15 foot rope, (I recommend soft Marine ½" Braided Nylon or Cotton Rope)
- Training surcingle/roller and elastic side reins
- Hip Pouch and supply of your horse's favourite treats. (You will note that I will occasionally stress the use of whole carrots for some tricks, this is purely to save bitten fingers as your horse tries to hold balance in a tricky position)
- Schooling Whips of various lengths
- Saddle & Bridle
- Clicker Box
- Patience of a Saint

For your horse's safety:-
- Protective Bandages or Boots
- Tail Bandage
- Well fitting and maintained tack

For your safety:-
- A well fitting riding hat that meets current approved safety standards.
- Gloves and Good Boots for protection and better grip.
- Body Protector, a wise precaution when training horses

Additional props and items used in this book!
- Large Ball
- Large Handkerchief
- Specially Constructed Pedestal
- Old Fashioned Bicycle Air Horn
- Large Soda Bottle
- Hat
- Old Phone
- Flag

Chapter 1: Back to Basics

17

There are no short cuts or quick fixes in horse training. It takes time, patience, effort and preparation to train any horse and the same principles apply when attempting the tricks and movements in this book.

To be successful you require a good understanding of how the horse learns and how they think. To achieve the level of communication you need to earn a place at the head of your horse's herd, you need to consider, learn, and practise the rules of Equus and horse psychology otherwise referred to as the science of 'Equine Ethology'.

Horses are simple, honest, genuine creatures. They love and crave social contact, food, play, quiet and wide open spaces. They also live in a very hierarchal structured herd environment that revolves around simple communication based on body language and respect for the herd leader. All of this can be manipulated by us in order to communicate to a far higher level than most of the horse community can dare or are even prepared to imagine.

Everything we have to teach them can already be found in the horse's natural behaviour, For instance they all know how to lie down, how to bow to reach that greener bit of grass under the fence, curling their upper lip to catch a strange smell on the breeze, the list goes on. What we need to do is to harness these behaviours on cue. To do this we first need to teach ourselves how to train a horse before we can hope to be completely successful with our equine students. Otherwise we are the blind leading the blind.

Understand Your Equine Friend!

Firstly you need to look at the world through your horses eyes. Your horse is a *'prey'* animal. They live in herds for protection, safety in numbers, and thrive on social contact.

To survive as a prey animal your horse has a deeply instilled trigger instinct to run first and think later. To your horse this is a matter of life and death, and we humans tend to play down this flight instinct in our horses as silliness and scold the horse for it because we do not react in the same way. Few of us stand back and question why our horse has reacted in that way! To your horse it is not simply a noisy plastic bag rustling in the hedge but a predator lurking in the undergrowth preparing to pounce.

Therefore before accepting anything that is strange or unusual to them they will at first retreat to a safe distance, usually at speed. Once satisfied that a safe distance has been reached they will then turn to face what it was they were running from. They will then apply an advance and retreat approach to investigate, until they are comfortable that there is no threat.

For instance, from a distance your horse spots a plastic bag lurking in the long grass, it has his interest but he is not quite sure what it is. If the horse has run away, he will stop as soon as he feels he is at a safe distance, he will then turn to face the object and raise his head and ears to survey the scene from afar. If nothing bad happens he will approach a little closer and stop again, maybe even retreating a few steps if it starts to rustle in the wind. Happy again he will approach a little closer. This advance and retreat will be repeated until the horse is sure there is no risk to his furry behind, until eventually he can stick his nose in the bag to investigate! The horse's entire life is governed by these survival instincts.

Humans on the other hand are hunter predators, and the natural enemy of any prey animal. Most people never consider this and are completely oblivious of the fact that every day they trigger defensive survival instincts in their horses. This culminates in behaviour that humans blindly label as a vice or naughtiness such as biting, kicking, bolting, bucking and rearing. These actions are in fact a prey animal's natural way of defending themselves and showing their distrust for the human's predatory approach to life.

Where prey animals are cautious in nature and use advance and retreat habits to investigate matters, humans, being top of the food chain, charge straight into everything they do without thinking and expect the poor horse to follow without question! We have a hard time comprehending what it must be like to be constantly fearing for our lives and being forever prepared to run from danger if the need arises. It is therefore understandable that our horses should not trust or be comfortable with normal human behaviour. Millions of years of evolution have programmed them to think this way and we will fail if we force our predatory attitude on to them. This is why we must learn how the horse behaves and thinks. We must adopt the same behaviour ourselves so our horses will learn to accept us as another member of the herd, and eventually a trusted herd leader, rather than a threatening predator who wants to do them harm or cause conflict

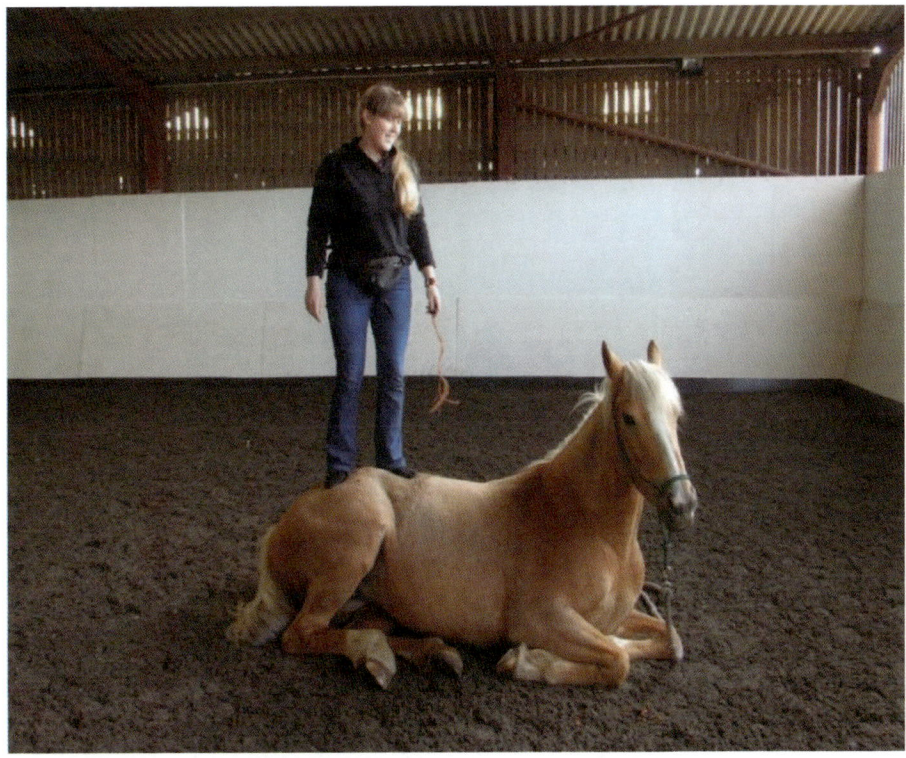

Above: Horse and owner fully focused and completely trusting in each other.

In bygone times horses were essential tools in farming, hunting, war and the creation of civilisation. It was vital to train the horse as quickly as possible, this meant that certain cultures began to introduce many shortcuts and equipment to speed up the training process which evolved into what I refer to as the 'old' or 'classical school'. In turn they sacrificed the gentle, magical relationship rarely attained these days. It can occasionally be seen in gifted 'horse whisperers' and those communities that still live in harmony with Mother Nature and all her gentle creatures. These people have stepped away from following quick but forceful methods and have seen better way of working with the horse and nature.

Throughout history such people were labelled 'Horse Whisperers' due to the lack of obvious visual communication. The masses could only assume that their skills with the horse were due to mystical, magical forces, and it was not uncommon for whisperers to be condemned as witches and often burned at the stake with their poor unfortunate horse. One such case was brought in 17th Century Arles France. The local witch hunters and god-fearing peasants condemned a performing trick horse called Mauroco with his Italian trainer in the town's market place. Their remarkable talents were considered so unusual that the only possible explanation was it must have been gifted through black magic and an unholy alliance with the devil.

Unfortunately such ignorance is not yet completely confined to the history books. People cannot accept that this can be learnt and can be the norm. If only more of the modern riding establishments would invest time in training their staff and pupils in Equus rather than in the use of whips, spurs, and elaborate tack!

Even today there is a lot of blind human arrogance in the way some trainers work. Some people believe that the horse must learn to accept the human way of life. After all, why should the humans change if they can beat, bully, force, or intimidate a defenceless animal into doing something their way! I personally find it unbelievable, ridiculous and indescribably frustrating that these people, of whom I have known many, believe themselves to be the intelligent being in the partnership.

Many individuals will not accept that they can use their bigger brain for a new way of thinking and a greater understanding of the horse as a unique individual with a different outlook on life. This would give them a huge advantage in their training. Learn to communicate as a prey animal rather than causing conflict and fear by scaring our sensitive equine partners with our predatory ways. If we can do this then we can compromise and work strongly together as partners.

This arrogant and forceful mentality leads to resentment from the horse and a lack of trust from both sides. I freely admit I was guilty of this same behaviour, I was taught as a child to pull on the reins to turn left and right, kick the horse to go, change to a stronger bit if I had trouble stopping, use the whip if the horse doesn't listen to the leg etc. Trouble is, this behaviour continues until we take the time to consider the alternatives. I am sure as a novice many people will have experienced these techniques at some level, whilst plodding round on a poor old pony that appears to have lost the will to live.

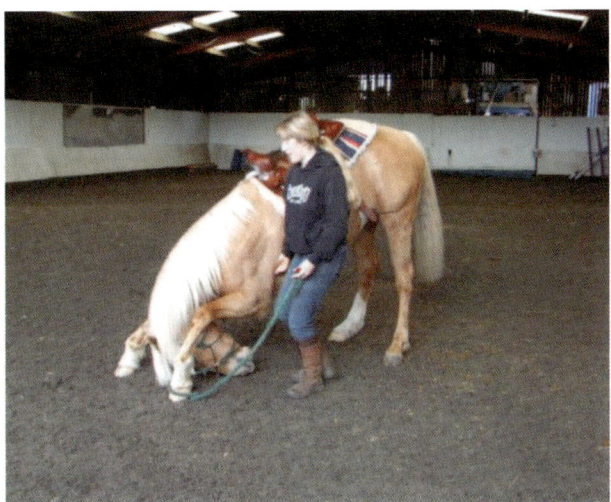 

Is there any harm in using equipment and extravagant tack if you know how to use them for extra control? Well, my answer to that is: 'Why do you need them in the first place?' Control and carriage can be established without these crutches and then only the simplest of equipment can be used later for polished refinement. To use them purely as a means of control the trainer must be compensating for something. It is usually the handler's lack of horsemanship. It's a fact that any horse can be taught to carry him-self well, and perform without fancy gadgets!

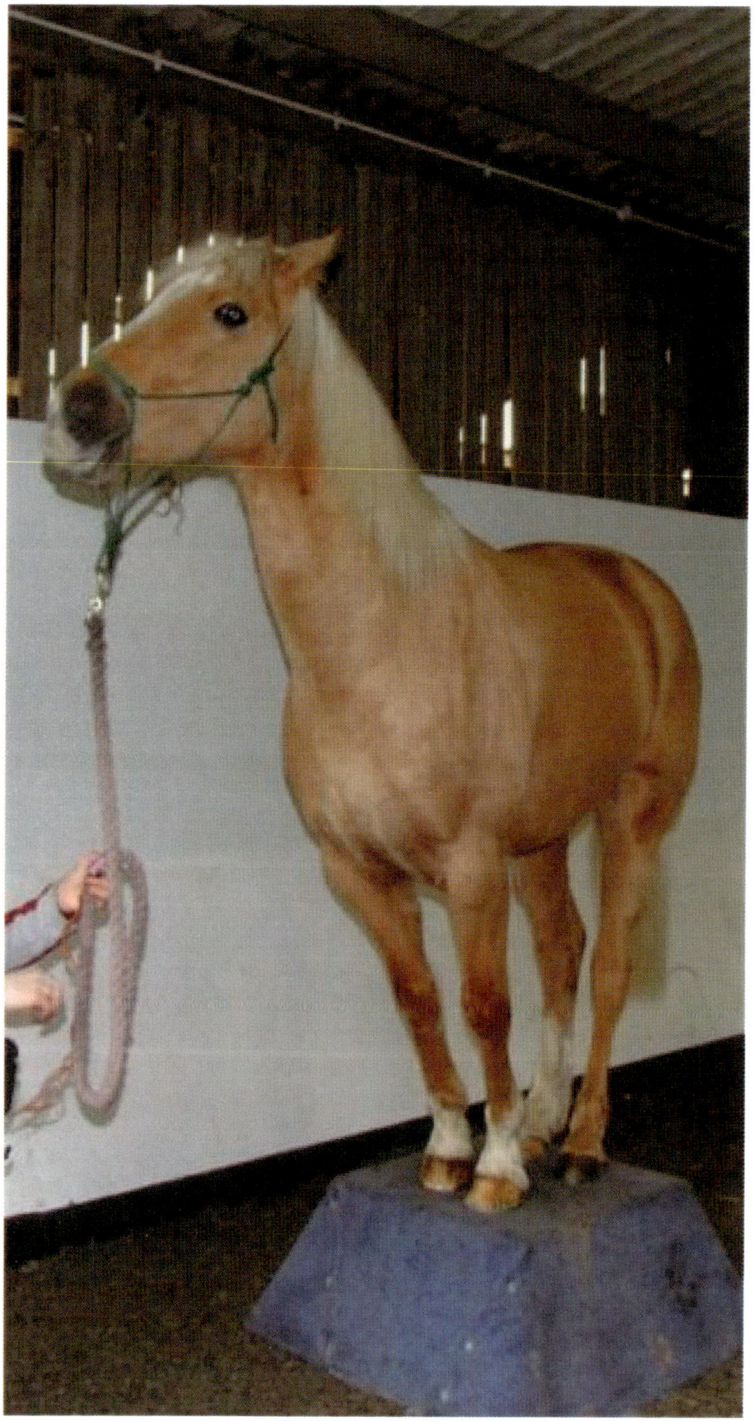

In addition to this some trainers believe that since domestication the horse has evolved to live in the human world! This is not the case. Horses are capable of learning to accept new environments, but it takes patience and sympathetic conditioning to produce such a horse. The horse's prehistoric instincts will always be lurking just below the surface ready to act unless you can understand what the horse is thinking. You can then support the horse accordingly!

Despite this and the horse's lot as a prey animal, they live their days in a very socially structured environment. Every horse has their place in herd hierarchy. Throughout their lives they are constantly battling within the herd to establish or improve their place in the pecking order, hopefully one day to become the head stallion or matriarchal mare. In the horse's eyes the human in their life must be tested in the same way. Unfortunately this is where many owners and riders lose control and respect. They get bullied by the horse. Add to this the human predatory approach and solutions and we have the recipe for disaster.

To gain social acceptance, trust and respect from our horses we must learn to understand, play, and win, the games horses understand to establish ourselves at the top of the pecking order.

If you can see the world from the horse's point of view you can understand it's main drives are safety, comfort, food and play. By using this horse psychology we can begin to establish an amazing and enviable relationship with our horses. We can banish the old school training methods of bullying horses into submission through, fear, intimidation, and elaborate artificial training aids and gadgets. These items are more commonly used for restraint that break and do so much damage to a horse's spirit, triggering the unwanted self defence behaviours so often seen. Instead, by using the natural approach and improving how we communicate, we can improve on the fragile relationship with our equine friends.

Through thoughtful natural communication and trick practice, we can begin to amazingly shape and mould our horse's behaviour. All we need is love, patience, and understanding. If we put the horse's feelings and well-being in front of our ultimate goals, our horses will in every case genuinely try their hardest to help and work with us as partners and indeed will enjoy doing so!

My point in this section is to make you aware how your horse views you and its surroundings, and how you as a person affect your horse's personality quite often without even realising it. Once you understand this, you should be able to see how this has a knock-on effect to your handling. You can then ensure training is hazard free with no distractions that will un-nerve your horse; like loud noises in the background, children squealing and running in and out of the school etc. You want to reassure your horse that they can concentrate on the learning and ensure they have not got half a mind to resort to natural flight mode because there is something that might startle them! You want your horse to feel safe in your company, and to believe that you wouldn't ask him to put himself into a situation where he could be surprised, placed in danger or hurt.

Always approach the training as if you were your horse's mother. Use gentle approach, retreat and yield to pressure methods to teach your student. Personally remain calm and never scold the horse or you will end up being labelled an untrustworthy predator that your horse wants to run away from. If your horses misbehave, ignore them, push them away as a mare would treat a foal and they will soon search for your attention and approval following you around like a shadow (otherwise known as join-up technique). A horse looking for your approval will approach cautiously with head lowered in a submissive posture and will chew or lick their lips like a foal, or minor herd member, does to a more dominant horse!

The secrets to a successful partnership with your horse are very simple, but it must be understood that they must be applied to every aspect of your horsemanship. This method although simple, takes time and patience, but the learning process accelerates at an unbelievable rate once the foundations of communication are truly understood by both teacher and student. *You will see a significant change in your horse as the light bulb flicks on between the ears when they finally understand the lessons.*

Even more amazing, your horse will try and communicate back by offering learned communications to show you what they want or if they need to grab your attention. You will be able to successfully read their character and body language and they will learn and act on yours. To experience this is truly amazing. I have described it to others as an almost spiritual connection with another creature, a language without words. Can you hear the whisper? You can if you truly want to!

Horses are extremely intelligent creatures and will surprise you. I recently experienced my horse trying to communicate that she wanted my attention. I had just completed a training session with her when I was interrupted by someone who needed to speak to me so my attentions were turned away from Fern. After nudging me repeatedly for attention from behind with no results she started to repeat the Bow lesson, which she had just been taught, both to my delight and my friend's surprise. She certainly got our attention which was what she was after.

So this only proves horses are capable of logical thought and communication. Fern knew what had pleased me 5 minutes earlier and logically if she wanted me to pay attention all she had to do was repeat the same thing!

Learn to be like your horse and your horse will love to learn! They are remarkable and will surprise you! You can even surprise yourself.

Can Any Horse Learn Tricks?

The answer is yes! Foals to mature horses can all learn something new. For the novice trainer, a sensible older horse is probably the best choice, as he will more than likely have a solid foundation in basic ground training and manners. Having a bit of life experience under his girth will also help him deal with new situations in a sensible manner. This will help the fledgling trainer concentrate on practising communication techniques without having an unpredictable nervous youngster to contend with.

Some older horses do have emotional & psychological baggage evolved purely through bad experience with humans. As far as they are concerned every human is the same until someone can prove to them otherwise. So this type of handling can go a long way to restoring trust and faith from our horses, a fragile and precious gift to be nurtured and treasured. However emphasis must be placed on restarting, re-educating, and establishing basic boundaries before concentrating on the majority of these tricks.

When they are introduced, always ensure that it is done gradually, and as a fun relaxing respite, complementing the horse's general schooling.

Once you have some training experience under your belt, you may want to take trick training a bit more seriously, in which case a young foal or yearling may be more appropriate. A young horse is like a blank unspoiled canvas for you to work your magic on, without the problems and issues that come with the average unsympathetically and traditionally trained horses. They learn quickly and their playful nature helps them progress as they learn to approach the training as if it was an enjoyable game. As a result, young horses that have been exposed to this type of learning stimulation at an early age grow up more intelligent, attentive, and easier to work with. They generally accept backing in their stride.

Youngsters are a pleasure to handle and learn at an accelerated rate as you have already established a firm foundation of understanding and communication. This type of training can also make good use of the early learning years when your youngster is not yet ready to take a rider and would otherwise spend most of his early life turned away with the exception of basic handling lessons. When the time eventually comes to take a rider the young trick horse will often accept this without batting an eye lid and can be a joy to work with. Foals can be handled sympathetically and gently from day of birth, but it is only around two months of age when they begin to become interested in solid foods and can be introduced to soft treat rewards such as peeled and chopped apple.

Whilst a horse's age is a big factor to consider, be aware that gender can considerably affect your horse's ability to perform. For the amateur trainer a mare or gelding is the wisest choice as they are not as difficult or as unpredictable as a stallion. However, if you wish to specialise in trick training, the stallion will undoubtedly have the boldest performance factor. Mares can be affected by their season cycles, and bouts of moody uncooperative behaviour can interrupt their concentration and routines. It is also the opinion of some, that a horse's ability to learn can be hindered after being gelded. This may or may not have a sound scientific explanation but may explain why so many dressage horses are left entire.

Horses with behavioural issues do benefit greatly from this training. As the nature of trick training is fun and unusual, you will find most horses with short attention spans, or those who have dulled to their normal routines, can soon be invigorated and enthusiastic about the new lessons. Horses that may be nervous, stressed or excitable will soon become laid back and thoughtful. Bossy and bullying types will learn their place in the horse-human pecking order, and the timid will come out of their shells and shine with confidence.

Whatever type, size or age of horse you choose, do take into consideration, their individual capabilities as well as your own. A senior horse may not be as nimble as he once was, and may find some of the tricks physically difficult, or perhaps even have accumulated some anti human issues that will take time to overcome. On the other hand a really young horse may also not be physically mature enough to take the stress of some of the more advanced tricks and will have a very short attention span. I will give some guidance on this throughout the book.

Analyse & Listen to Your Horse

28

To get the most from any horse, a good trainer must be familiar with their horse's personality, likes, dislikes, fears, talents, physical attributes, temperament, fitness and odd little quirks. The teacher can then tailor the lessons to get the most from their student, helping to develop the individual's abilities and nurture and work with his natural instinct and behaviours. You can also identify and target your horse's weaknesses or problem areas and focus on improving these through specific training exercises whilst building on your bond of trust, security and leadership.

Spend time quietly observing your horse, perhaps at play in the field, or interacting with other horses. Study his reactions to strange objects, and other people. How laid back or stressed is he in different situations, where does your horse feel most relaxed and comfortable when you are working together?

Consider which of the three natural instincts, 'Prey', 'Flight', or 'Herd', is strongest in your horse by how frequently he might react in different situations. Once you are familiar with your horse's personality you will be prepared to deal with training issues and problems if indeed they occur.

Which of the three following basic instinct behaviours your horse will adopt in any given situation, greatly depends on your horses history, upbringing and past experiences. Being able to identify his response will greatly improve your chance to predict problems before they occur and prepare accordingly.

By noting what motivates him you can use this knowledge to make training sessions more fun and interesting. Recognize what alarms him and you can prepare for it, taking the time to reassuringly work it through with him. Understand how he behaves with other horses and use this to gain his respect and social acceptance as a kind herd leader whom he loves to spend time with and will follow without question. Study what motivates him (usually food!) and you are set to provide the ideal motivation when needed! Horses can be strongly affected by all the following instincts.

1. Prey- The prey animal instinct is what defines your horse, a creature that in a natural lifestyle is driven to seek out and graze for food stuffs. Horses that have a strong Prey instinct love their grub! Being highly motivated by food means the horse will be very easy to train through treat rewards. It can also mean a cheeky personality which will need keeping in check.

- Is your horse protective of his dinner or does he bolt his food?
- Does your horse like to take things in his mouth and chew on everything?
- Does he pull at the lead or stretch under the fence for some grass

2. Flight- Is the self preservation instinct. Presented with a stressful, startling or unusual situation, the horse will turn and take flight, a run first think later reaction. How secure, confident or timid is your horse?
- Does your horse jump at the paper wrapper in the hedge and turn on his heels to run home?
- Does he run to the back of the stable when you approach?
- Is he difficult to catch?
- Is he a bag of nerves in traffic, near strange objects or strange noises?
- Does he dislike being handled, touched, groomed or petted?

A horse that has a strong flight instinct is often quite nervous, tense and easily stressed. Therefore you need to work on trust and convincing your horse that you will protect and keep them safe so they can learn to chill and relax. Consistency in your instructions, a slow calm reassuring manner and a safe & quiet working environment are paramount when dealing with flight instinct as concentration is often difficult for such animals.

3. Herd- Defines the horse's social abilities and willingness to interact with both horses and humans. This encompasses herd pecking orders, dominance and respect issues as well as communication and leadership games.
- Is your horse social with other horses, does he like to play and groom with others, call out to his friends or run around when his field mates are removed?
- Is he affectionate to you? Does he follow you closely, welcome you with a whinny, or enjoy you petting him or scratching his itchy spot?

- How dominant is he, is he the field bully or does he get picked on by other horses? Is he cheeky, bolshie or dangerous with his handler or does he do what he is asked with no fuss with a happy ears forward outlook?

Horses demonstrating strong herd behaviours love the company of others, and will relish the extra attention they get in their training. They enjoy being in a social environment and interacting with other horses or people. They miss their field companions if left alone and will greet you when you arrive. It is in their nature to create strong bonds and this can be used to great advantage when trying to establish a strong partnership with your beloved horse! Such horses also test their social standing in the herd on a regular basis which means they will regularly challenge your authority as leader so you have to be ready for such situations.

As a general rule, concentrate on the instinct strongest in your horse, and tailor the training accordingly. Ensure you don't ignore the part the other behaviours play in your horse's behaviour, always adjusting the lessons to suit the situation. Prey horses train well with food treats, Flight animals need a quiet area to work and focus, Strong herd instinct means extra quality time and plenty of praise, cuddles and pats from you as herd leader, etc.

Horses communicate through body language. These signs of communication vary from the very obvious to the extremely subtle. If you do not give 101% of your absolute undivided attention to your horse you will miss what your horse has to say to you! For example your horse is uncomfortable having his tummy brushed and kicks out at you. Did you notice or listen to the mounting ways he was trying to tell you, the swishing tail, the ears pinned back, the bobbing of the head then him trying to turn to nip you. Or did he just get shouted at to stand still and be good. You need to listen and react to everything he tells you in order to have a two way communication as partners.

You also have to be fully aware of your own behaviour as it can have such a significant impact on your horse without you even knowing it! Unfortunately as the human is a hunter predator any unconscious human habits only result in negative and conflicting responses from the horse. Therefore as the 'more intelligent' partner we must put aside our predatory habits and adopt the thinking of the horse to enable us to guide our furry friends and avoid hunter/prey conflicts arising.

In the same way we analyse the horse we can and should regularly take an honest look at ourselves to identify hunter predator behaviours in us that will affect and undoubtedly cause conflict in our relationship with the horse. It can be beneficial to ask another person for their opinion on how you rate on a predatory instinct scale. The following notes summarise some of the pros and cons these cause when dealing with a prey animal such as the horse.

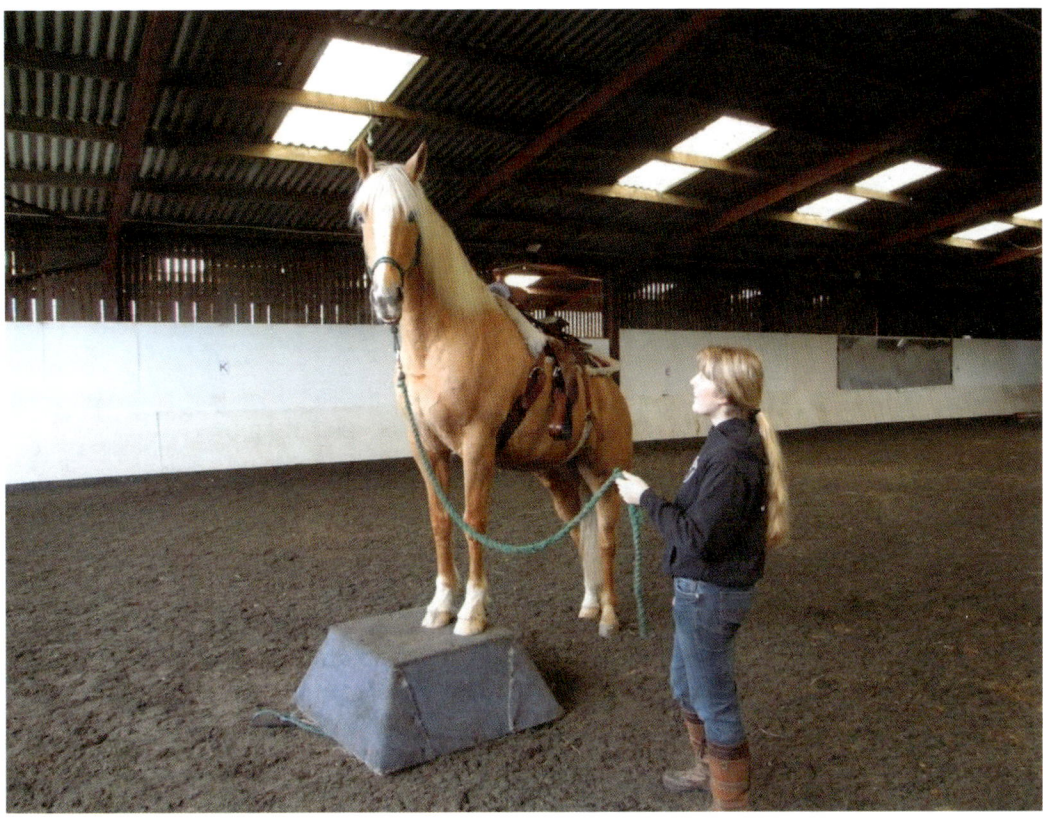

1. Predator Instinct- Like the horses Prey instinct, this is the human drive to hunt and feed. We have the ability to maintain lengthy periods of concentration when working and stalking prey. Horses on the other hand tend to lose interest in things before we do. Also, our scope of vision is limited compared to the horses, something can startle a horse we haven't even seen or noticed. Then finally our natural mannerisms and movement are the complete opposite of the horse. Our tendency to march straight into situations, to grab for things and then hold on for grim death is like a pouncing and aggressive predator.

2. Fight Instinct- Generally humans stand and confront threats to our safety and if necessary will physically try and defend ourselves. As a hunter race this was necessary for our survival in prehistoric times in the hunt for large prey for the cave larder. As we are the hunters and top of the food chain, we will charge into any situation without too much concern for our mortal safety. Horses on the other hand will take flight and when they instinctively want to run for survival, we try and hold them back wanting them to stay and fight alongside us which the poor horse is not programmed to do! If you are a fighter you need to work on understanding your horse's nature, otherwise you will end up always fighting with your horse and triggering self defence and flight reactions in the poor creature. The timid or nervous among us can perhaps sympathetically identify with the horse in this matter.

3. Social- Like the horses herd instinct, humans tend to live in family groups, normally with a parent at the head of the family. Some people relish company and dealing with other people through work etc, others cannot stand company and prefer to be left alone. Everyone challenges the human social structure on a daily basis, whether it is arguing with parents or trying to climb the corporate ladder at work. It is therefore natural that your horse does the same and will challenge you. You need to learn how to always win the challenges to hold your horse's respect, but should not blame your horse for trying! Socially you must also consider how much quality time you spend with your horse. If you are not one to hand out pats and cuddles, and your horse likes such attention then maybe you should be going 50:50.

By listening and observing you can identify the key instinct and qualities that make your horse tick. Without being aware of what's normal behaviour for your equine friend, you will be completely oblivious to what he has to say and his personal needs and you won't be effective in your training. Your horse speaks to your every time you are with him, but do you truly listen to him or even recognise when he is trying to communicate?. This is the true nature of whispering! You have to pay attention, observe and listen or you will miss what is being said and will be unable to apply your knowledge of the horse's instincts to communicate and reassure.

Allowed to express his true personality your horse will enjoy your company and his work. A horse having fun in his job, puts his all into every task and you will see the fun and enthusiasm in your horse's eyes, energy, confidence and presence. It's a joy to see, and should be a reflection on the time, love and patience you have spent on your friend!

Remember to Say Sorry!

33

We all make mistakes from time to time and this includes both horses and humans alike. The important thing in any relationship is to own up and admit your mistake and apologise to the loved one we hurt or upset. You may have heard the saying 'Never go to bed angry!' This is very true and you must never put your horse away on a bad note.

If your horse doesn't get the lesson you have been working on and you start getting flustered or upset, stop and go to a trick your horse knows well. Reward for performing the familiar trick and then put your horse away on the good note. Your horse can then think over the lesson with good memories and you can then rethink your method and try again another day.

Horses are very forgiving animals. They put us to shame in this respect. They put up with a lot from us humans. Occasionally they stand up for themselves only to get more of the same from us and a telling off simply for trying to defend themselves from impatient unsympathetic bullies that call themselves trainers.

If you make an error whilst training or you accidentally poke you horse or jab him in the mouth. Stop immediately and make your apologies. Rub it better and give him a hug, tell him you're sorry and give him a bit of love and you will find he will drop his head to you to say you are forgiven.

However continue to make the same mistake, or take your frustrations out on your horse, and you will end up with problems and a horse that is fearful, uncooperative and dull to your instructions.

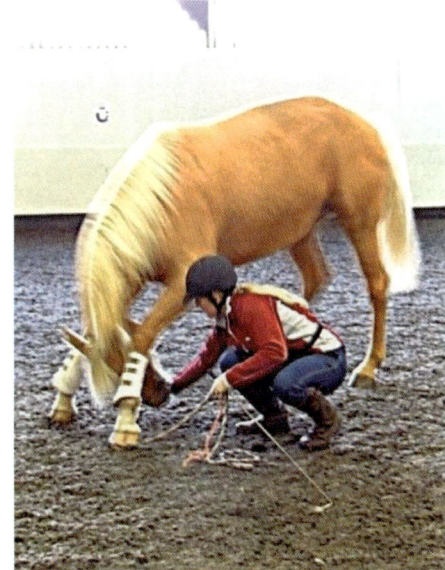

Golden Rules to Successful Trick Training

Keep yourself on the fast track to training success. The following notes should be followed as a general rule whenever you handle and train your horse.

- Keep training sessions short, horses do not have a long attention span and can bore easily, plus long sessions can cause tiredness and stress. This rule will vary depending on the individual horse, for instance youngsters and seniors will tire quicker and youngsters tend to be more easily distracted and bored. Restrict the time spent on each session, do not endlessly repeat movements as this can be punishing to the horse.

- Be consistent in your training sessions and commands, so the horse can learn to read you and your body language. Horses learn to predict your actions, therefore if you are clear and consistent your horse will soon pick up what you are asking of them. It will also ensure your horse feels more secure and confident around you, as they will find it easier to understand behavioural boundaries and what is expected of them.

- Make the reward worth the effort. Always keep your promise of reward if used as an incentive. The horse is more likely to try harder for the treat before his tea than after, or crave your attention more just after you have brought him in from the field rather than after a long ride and grooming session. Timing of reward is essential in reinforcing positive and good behaviours.

- Always remain calm, be patient and respectful, exactly how you wish your student to behave towards you. Horse temperaments and behaviours often reflect those of their owners and sometimes past handlers.

- Remember it takes as long as it takes, every horse is an individual and will learn at their own speed. As you progress your will find your horse starts to learn quicker as you develop your lines of communication. Note: - it is quite often found that those animals that pick up bad habits, vices, and like to test your patience a lot, are the most intelligent and capable.

- Break tricks down into to manageable training steps, and ensure your horse can happily complete stage one before you confront them with stage two. Remember students can feel demoralised if they don't feel they are getting anywhere and you will just get frustrated. By breaking lessons down to achievable goals your horse is more likely to want to try, rather than become fearful of failing and disappointing you.

- Never reward behaviour that you have not requested. Your goal is to obtain obedience on cue, not just when the student feels like it. Try to ignore any undesirable behaviour, blanking your horse is usually enough to show your displeasure, this is the natural punishment dispensed in the herd environment, anything further will lead to problems and potentially damage your student's spirit. If your horse is really misbehaving and not just confused or frightened by a situation give your horse the cold shoulder until he behaves and then invite him back into your space once the behaviour is acceptable.

- Ensure when working with your horse, that he feels comfortable in his lesson environment, and that there is little around to distract or spook him. You want him to completely relax and focus on you, not what is happening in the next field. You may not want an audience until the horse is happy doing the trick in your company, if he trusts you completely he is more likely to perform when you ask him to in front of others. Sadly, this can be near to impossible in today's over crowded livery yards, so if this is a problem ensure people know you require 10 minutes peace before you start to give you both a chance to concentrate.

- Horses like to learn and follow, but they must first respect their teacher and leader. Always be fair and just in all that you ask, and the horse will genuinely try his best for you.

- When going about your daily business try and expose the horse to new sights, sounds and smells. If your horse finds something alarming do not try and avoid it, but give your horse time to investigate it for themselves so next time they won't bat an eyelid! Turning tail and fleeing from such events just reinforces your horse's natural instinct to run by following the leader! The horse will be thinking that 'my brave leader walked away and I am feeling a little unsure and scared, so then it cannot be a good thing, I will run away too!'

- Always work your horse in the minimum amount of equipment you need to get the job done. As the horse improves you will find you can discard quite a bit of equipment for example additional guidance ropes etc. Constantly adjust the amount of equipment used in each lesson so your horse does not associate a particular trick with certain pieces of equipment.

- Stopping an aid or stimulation at the correct time when the horse has tried to offer you something close to the correct behaviour will teach the horse he has done well. Don't nag! Stop when you have the slightest 'try' and tell the horse he has been good before trying again. Just think! You would soon start to ignore someone nagging you when you had done as you had asked but the effort had gone unnoticed & unappreciated.

- Don't actively restrict and restrain your horse's movements, but use opposition reflex conditioning to improve the situation. Restraining a panicking horse from moving his feet will aggravate the horse's claustrophobic nature and they will panic even more. Working your horse on a long line will give him a chance to get over a flighty panic attack before you run out of rope.

- Imagine you are now the student, you suffer from a highly nervous constitution and are an extremely sensitive individual, easily alarmed, jumpy and subject to panic attacks, you are now faced with a loud, insensitive teacher who is yelling non-stop instructions at you in a second language and nagging you to do it again and again when you thought you had already given it a good try... How do you feel? ...You are now in your horse's shoes!

- The one who controls the situation is in charge! If your horse is pushing you around, you're not at the top of the pecking order. Make sure you practice manoeuvring your horse by applying pressure to drive the horse in every direction; this affirms your authority and also helps to teach the horse to respect your space.

- The horse is not conscious of his physical strength until the force of a human tests it. Therefore always handle you horse in a manner that won't give him the opportunity to test his muscle!

- Horses examine the world through sight, sound, smell and touch, so by allowing your horse the freedom to exercise his senses freely he will accept anything you ask of him.

- Your horse wont resist any lesson if it is taught in a manner sympathetic to his natural instincts

37

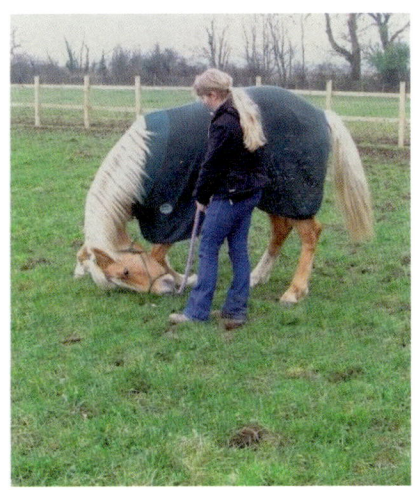

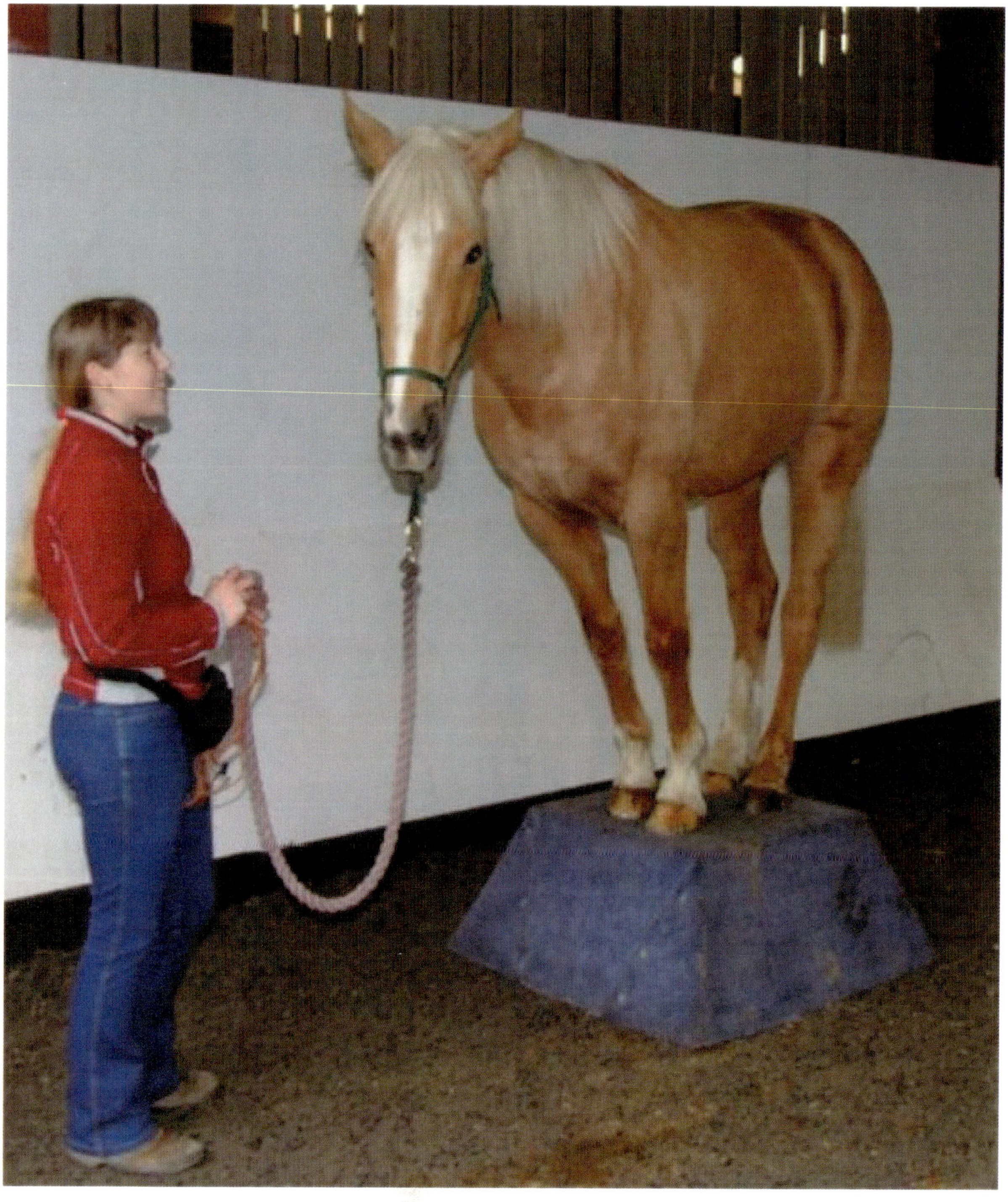

Trick or Treat

It is important to consider the subject of treats and rewards carefully. To reward your student for an action or behaviour that is desired can speed up the learning process dramatically. If used only when the student has acted correctly they will soon begin to think about and question what they just did that earned them that reward, and so strive to repeat and improve on the performance, responding quicker and eventually on cue. Your horse will also begin to think of performing very much as a way to train you to produce a treat!

Timing is also critical. Generally you should apply a 3 second rule so your horse will associate the reward with the action. Any longer than this and you can lose the thought connection between trick and treat.

Rewards are not only limited to food! That tasty morsel can be crucial in prompting desired behaviour in the beginning, but if you are not careful it can lead to a greedy pushy animal unless used with good timing and moderation. Once general behaviour is established it can be wise to move to physical reward, such as scratching your horse's favourite itchy spot, verbal praise, or simply putting the horse back in his field to relax and contemplate his lesson over a juicy blade of grass or two!

If you keep a firm but gentle downward pressure on the rope the horse will at first show an opposition reflex and try and raise his head, However if you keep the pressure constant the horse will find it uncomfortable and eventually try to relieve the discomfort by lowering the head. The second the horse does what you have asked you must release the pressure as a 'comfort' reward, So, the horse learns that by lowering his head and giving to the pressure as soon as you ask he has relieved his discomfort and arrived in a 'comfortable place'. Repeating this exercise will reinforce your horse understanding until he yields to the slightest hint of pressure immediately.

Alternatively if the horse does what you ask and you do not release the pressure this will cause frustration and resentment on the part of the horse and he will just learn to ignore you because you do not acknowledge his efforts.

During training it is best to have several levels of verbal praise, ranging from a reassuring 'Good Boy' and a gentle pat or scratch to acknowledge a step in the right direction or slightest effort, right up to going potty with prolonged and excessive praise, upping the volume telling him what a clever and brilliant guy he is, hugging and scratching all the right places and emptying your treat bag for him.

If you give the same level praise for everything, your horse will not know if he is doing right, going wrong, or if he has hit the nail on the head and given a brilliant performance. He is also liable to ignore repetitive 'good boys' if they have no meaning behind them. Your tone of voice can reflect degrees of affection, excitement, encouragement, and warmth, so use this to your advantage when working with your horse! He is an enthusiastic kid who wants to make you proud of him, talking to him in this nurturing, encouraging, and enthusiastic way may sound silly but he will love you and flourish on it!

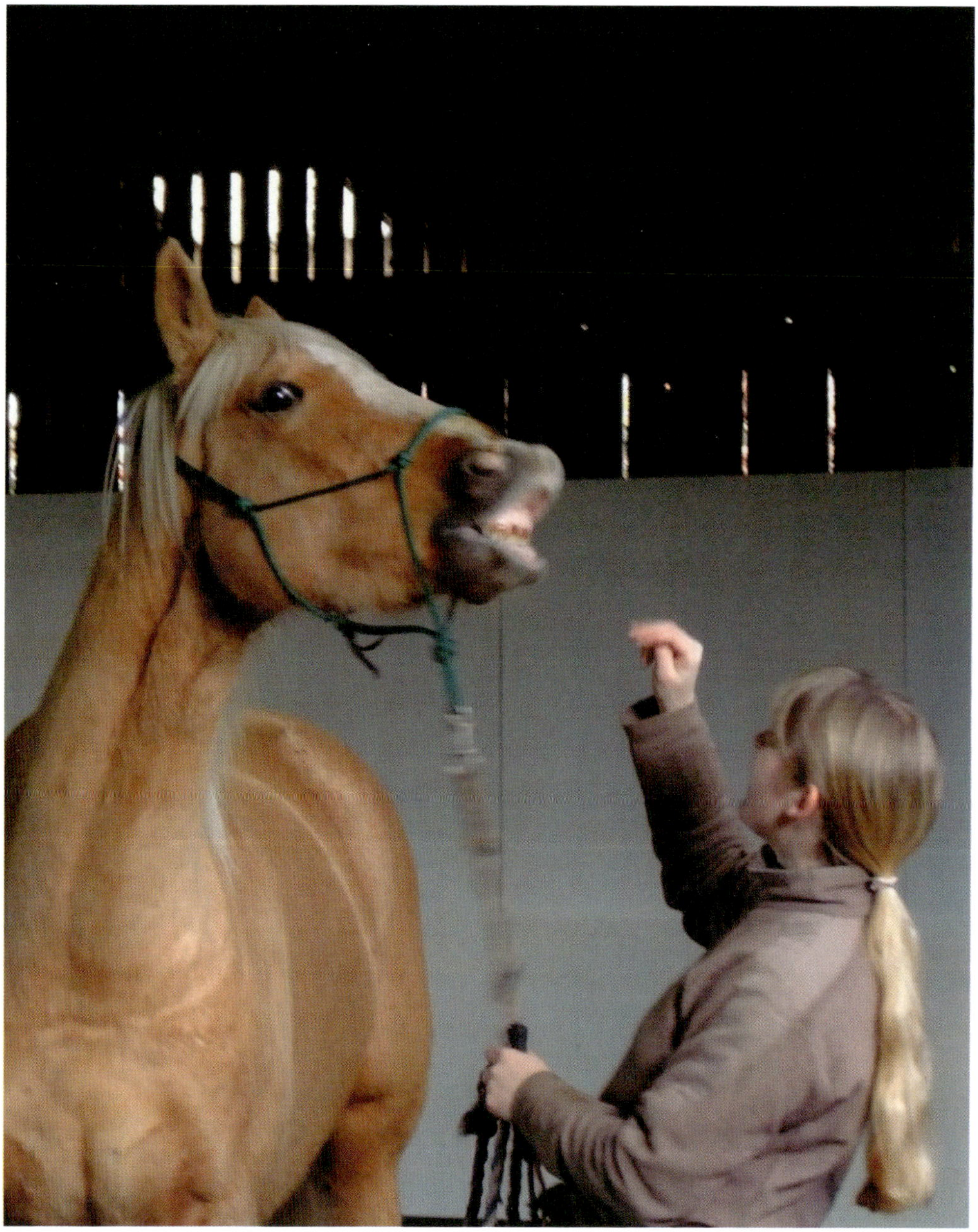

Take great care not to praise or reward for mediocre or sloppy behaviour or manners, this is in effect fibbing to your horse. Rewarding only when he has been good or fantastic will give your horse confidence. Lavish the praise, attention and rewards that your horse loves and craves to guide him to a perfect performance.

Another form of reward is the use of a 'Clicker Box'. This is a small plastic box that omits a clicking noise when pressed. Originally developed as an aid to train dolphins it has been adopted as a positive reinforcement technique for horses. It has proven a great success for shaping good behaviour and is ideal for telling the horse immediately when they have given you the correct answer.

Training Tip: - If you have concerns regarding your horse becoming nippy training with food treats, the simple answer, which many people do not think of, is don't feed the treats from your hand. Give a click or pile on the praise & hugs to acknowledge your horse's efforts, but then toss the treat on the ground or into a bucket so the horse isn't taking them directly from your hand. This stops the horse looking for and grabbing at your person for treats. After hearing the click your horse is more likely to go and wait by his bucket for a treat to appear. Problem solved!

Challenge Your Imagination

To keep life interesting for both our horses and ourselves we need to set ourselves challenges and goals. By pushing the boundaries and exploring new ideas, the training possibilities are only limited by our imaginations. We are then on the correct path to discover exactly what is possible and exactly what our horses are capable of.

Remember once you have taught your horse a simple trick or aid, there is always another level you can take it to. This will add challenge and interest to your lessons. For instance, you teach your horse to Bow from the ground, you can progress onto practising in the saddle, how about then trying bare back, or maybe without a bridle as well, the list goes on.

Don't be afraid of trying new things and methods and never settle for mediocre or second best when it comes to training your horse. If your horse won't walk past a tractor without panicking or takes an hour to load on a trailer, are you really happy with this? You need to use your imagination and set yourself the challenge to work on and improve such problems.

By using the simple techniques in this book you will soon learn how to introduce your horse to new things and gently and methodically shape your horse behaviour for practical and more imaginative purposes whilst having fun together!

Below: You'll both learn to trust each other and attempt new things.

Chapter 2: Laying Good Foundations

Before I begin with the trick lessons, I want to share with you some basic handling techniques and the philosophy that you have to understand to make your horsey training a lot easier.

To progress quickly and be successful you will require a sound foundation to your training and relationship. Without solid and good foundations a building will crumble, cracks will begin to develop, and eventually the building will fall or have severe structural problems making any future development impossible, dangerous, or at least very shaky. The same can be said about the partnership you wish to develop with your horse.

Horses naturally play games to establish a pecking order in their herds. The better they are at winning these games the closer to the top of the herd they will get. Therefore if you want to be top of the herd in your horse's eyes, you need to play the same games with your horse and win every time!

In this chapter I summarise a number of lessons or games as the horse understands them. These games help to establish you at the top of the herd and will help you polish your basic communication skills. You will be a fair and gentle leader your horse can confidently, respectfully, and attentively follow and learn from. Master these lessons and the tricks will be easy!

You will also need a way of communicating to your horse when he has done well which is where I advocate the use of a clicker box and I will show you how to establish a link in your horse's mind that when he hears the clicker he knows he has done well.

Yielding to Pressure

Teaching your horse to yield to pressure should be one of the most important parts of his basic training. If a horse is not taught to give or move away from pressure they will instinctively fight against it. It is an invaluable teaching exercise that trains your horse to avoid discomfort by giving to any pressure aid as soon as possible rather than fighting it. This results in not only an easier relaxed life for him, but pleases you in the process.

Most horses you will meet today are resistant to pressure in some way, and this causes stressful problems for themselves and irritable handlers that lose their horses respect because they don't know how to correct the behaviour without applying further force. For instance I am sure you will know horses that ignore leg aids, horses that lean on or evade the bit, pull on their halters, or try and set their head and necks against you and bolt off!

All of these situations are examples of horses who fight pressure and have lost respect for their owners. This is usually the result of owners

ignoring or missing the slightest efforts their horses have made in the early period of training, constantly nagging for the perfect performance first time rather than rewarding the slightest try in the right direction. They have also learnt their own strength because a human has tested theirs against the horse and failed miserably!

Imagine you are having a riding lesson and your teacher asks you to do something new and unfamiliar to you. You are unsure but give it your best shot anyway, the result isn't fabulous but the basics are obviously there! You look towards your teacher for acknowledgement and encouragement that you are on the right track. You get absolutely no feedback, but asked to do it again and again and again, which you do but as you don't know what you have got right or wrong you can only repeat what you did the last time only to get yelled at again. Eventually the nagging drives you up the wall and you give up and start to blank the teacher or maybe even start to argue and defend yourself. How many horses do you think suffer the same at the hands of unsympathetic handlers?

To truly have a dream horse that is a joy to own and happy in his work he must first understand and accept this training and you must also fully understand how to teach and work with it. Once your horse has successfully accepted the training, your horse will be light to handle, attentive, eager to please, confident, relaxed and ready to learn anything.

The training will also help establish you as a herd leader, that your horse respects, can trust implicitly, and can follow and look up to for comfort, reassurance and guidance. As I mentioned earlier, it is your horse's natural instinct to constantly test your leadership to try and improve their social standing in the herd. This is the method that will earn you the respect and help you to hold your place as herd leader in your horse's eyes.

Tools required: - Head Collar, Lead Rope, Treat Bag & Treats, and Schooling Whip

To begin your 'Yield to Pressure' lessons and possibly your horse's first true lesson in submission, dress your horse in a head collar (preferably a string pressure halter), long lead rope and carry a little hoard of treats. The first lesson will be to teach your horse to give to pressure placed on the head. Normally if you pull forward or downward on your lead rope the horse's immediate reaction would be to pull upwards or backwards even if it is only slightly. This is a natural opposition reflex.

Next stand at your horse's shoulder and place your hand just below the clip of the lead rope. Start applying a gentle steady downward pressure on the rope, slowly increasing the pressure, you can also give a verbal cue if desired such as 'down'. As soon as the horse gives the slightest try, it is extremely important you release the rope immediately and reward with lots of praise, cuddles and treats. By doing this you have rewarded the horse by releasing the pressure that was causing him discomfort, by praising, and also by treating as soon as he gave you the right answer. Your horse should suddenly twig, 'I can fight, and give myself a sore head and nose, or, I can give as soon as the pressure starts and get rewarded for it. The method of gradually increasing the pressure also helps the horse under-stand, the quicker they comply the quicker they are rewarded and avoid greater discomfort. Soon the slightest downward pressure on the lead will get your horse to drop his head immediately or follow as soon as you ask.

It will take several lessons for your horse to understand completely so be patient and give him plenty of encouragement. You can then start to apply these principles to teach your horse new things, such as moving away from leg pressure or backing up from gentle pressure on the nose etc.

Introducing Clicker Training

The clicker box is the perfect tool to deliver an immediate and consistently recognisable acknowledgement that your horse has done well. The clicker is an ingenious device that uses positive reinforcement techniques to methodically shape your horse's behaviour.

To begin using the clicker you must start with an easy lesson. For this example I am going to combine the introduction of the clicker with another valuable training lesson 'Learning to Target'.

Targeting teaches the horse to focus on and follow a target and can be incredibly useful when you require your horse to focus on something to prevent him worrying about other things. An example of this is asking the horse to follow the target up a trailer ramp; the horse concentrates on the target and not the trailer.

Tools Required: Head collar, Lead rope, Clicker box, Bag of Treats, Target Stick

Lesson 1: Dress your horse in a head collar and tie him up loosely with the rope so he can move his head. Next hold the ball end of your target stick under his nose for him to investigate. On the first sign of him sniffing or even touching the ball with his muzzle, click immediately, reward and praise him well.

Lesson 2: Repeat lesson one until you horse clearly understands that by just touching the target ball he will receive a click from your box, a yummy treat and lots of praise and attention.

Lesson 3: Keep practising lesson two but begin to move the target around for your horse to follow, as soon as his nose hits the target he will get the click and reward.

Stand Still & Correct

Not a trick as such, but a fantastic way of showing your horse off at his best, and it is without doubt one of the most important and practical lessons you can teach your horse!

Fantastic for the show ring poser or the animals that just won't stand still! It not only prepares the horse to catch a judge's eye, but it is also teaches your horse patience and discipline whilst standing absolutely still, square & correct.

This training should have many applications and I believe should be used as a preparation before teaching other tricks to get the horse concentrated, quiet, and listening and focused on what is to follow. As a simple safety measure, a horse that stands still when requested and won't budge until told to do so is obviously worth its weight in gold.

Tools required: - Head Collar, Lead rope, Clicker, Treats & Schooling Whip

Lesson 1:- Start by asking your horse to stand square. To do this you should stand directly in front of your horse and hold the head by taking hold of the cheek pieces on the halter or bridle. Adjust your horse's stance by pulling gently as necessary on the cheek pieces to encourage the legs level. After adjusting your horse's position clearly ask the horse to 'Stand'. Click, praise and reward as soon as the horse is in the desired position.

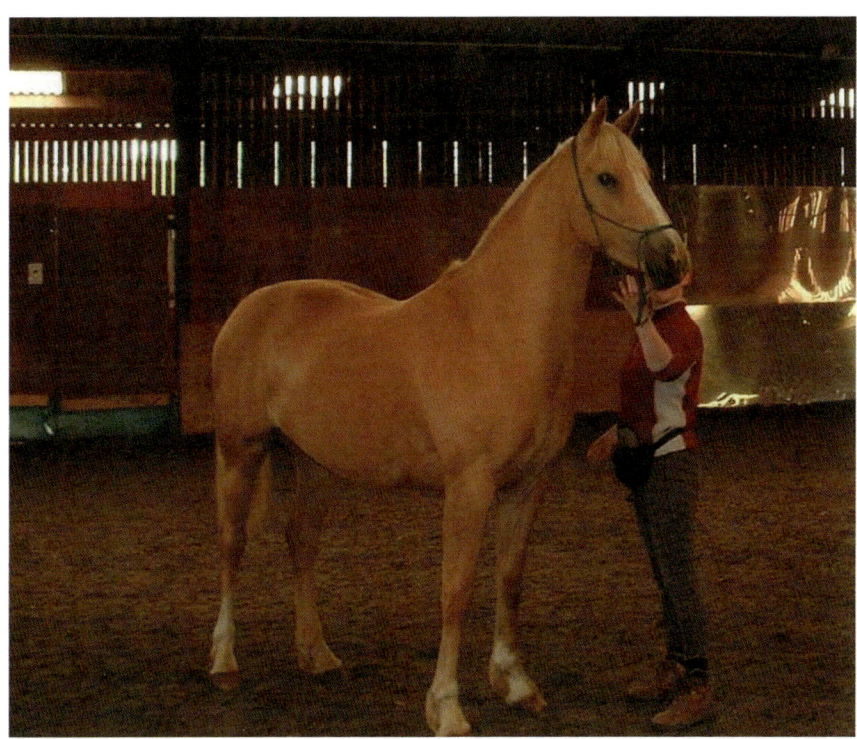

Lesson 2:- Now the horse is square, stand at your horses shoulder and raise your horse's head with your hand under the horse's jaw as per the photo. Ask you horse to 'Stay', hold the head for a couple of seconds and then give a click on the clicker or say 'Good Boy' and follow it up with a treat.

Lesson 3:- Repeat lesson 2, your horse should hold the pose until he hears a click. Next, slowly start to remove your hand, from under the chin whilst repeating the verbal cue 'stay'. If the horse moves, reposition the head and start again. Only reward when your horse holds the position until hearing the click.

Lesson 4:- Repeat lesson 3 until your horse holds the pose whilst you can stroke him on the neck for a few seconds. Insist he doesn't move until hearing the click.

Lesson 5:- Repeat this training in stages until you can walk all the way around your horse and back to his head again without him moving a whisker. This will be an achievement because you will note as you progress that your horse will be itching to move but with practice will eventually hold out for the sound of the clicker.

Lesson 6:- Once you complete lesson 5, you can play with this trick to see how far you can retreat from your horse without them moving or following until invited to do so!

Training Tip

For horses that won't stand still whilst mounting, grooming, hosing etc. Master this lesson and you will make life a whole lot easier for yourself. Ensure you click, praise and reward him well when he complies and he will soon learn to stand still whenever you ask!

The trick to get your horse to stand still is learning to hold your horse's attention. It is very difficult to keep horses focused and listening to you. As you work through the lesson, keep talking to your horse. When the horse is focused on you his ears will follow you as you move around. Keep talking and repeating the command whilst praising as you go! Your horse will eventually be so focused he will remain statuesque until he hears the clicker or a verbal 'Good Boy!'

Back Up

I like to teach this as part of my horse's foundation training as it instils in them a respect for your space and is essentially useful in day to day handling & manners. By wiggling the rope you transmit increasing energy to the horses halter until he moves backwards. When he complies he is rewarded by an immediate stop to the signals in the rope. This exercise also teaches your horse to listen to and recognise subtle signals and shows you how to manipulate the horse's position through dominant body language and positive reinforcement.

Tools Required: - Head Collar, Long Lead Rope, Whip or Training Stick & Treats

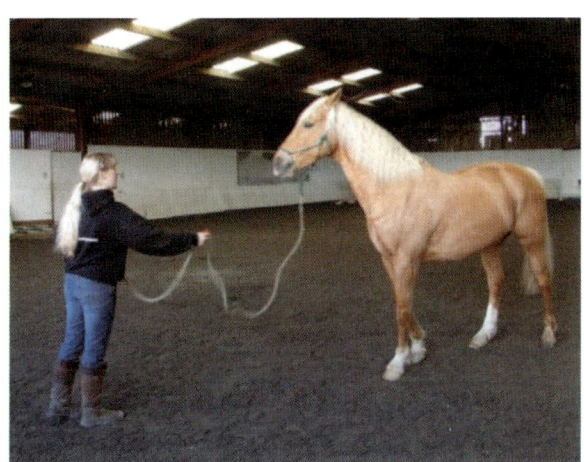

Lesson 1:- Dress you horse in a string halter and lead and stand directly in front of him. Holding the lead in one hand and the whip in the other, encourage the horse to move backwards by pushing gently but firmly with your stick in the centre of the horse's chest whilst at the same time wiggling the lead and saying 'Backup!'. Gradually increase the wiggle in the rope followed by the pressure on the chest until the horse finds it uncomfortable and steps backwards. As soon as the horse makes the slightest attempt to move backwards cease the wiggling and chest pressure immediately and treat and praise the horse for doing as asked.

Lesson 2:- Repeat the above exercise but try to do each aid methodically, A) Say 'Backup', (If no response) B) Say 'Backup' and wiggle rope, (If no response again) C) Say 'Backup', wiggle the rope harder and gesture toward the chest with the stick applying light pressure as necessary. Eventually the horse will realise that complying with your request earlier rather than later will avoid the uncomfortable steps and get a quicker reward.

Lesson 3:- Once your horse is moving backwards only on the word 'Backup', or on the lightest wiggle of the rope, practise to see how many steps backward you can make the horse take. Aim for 10, then anything more is a bonus!

Lesson 4:- Once happy with steps 1 to 3, remove the head collar and try again. This time try and imitate the body language you would have used if the rope and whip was still there, your horse should actually recognise the simple gesture of wiggling your hand as you did with the rope and respond accordingly. This body language with the word 'Backup' should now be enough to encourage the horse backwards.

Circle Away

50

Asking your horse to listen and yield to your body language is a beneficial lesson! This is a perfect trick to teach a horse to respect your space. You can also use this to practice your driving and pressure techniques and assert your dominance as herd leader whilst building on a system of respect and understanding. It is also a fantastic introduction to sending your horse away from you and asking for him to return to you on request.

Tools Required: - Head Collar, Long Lead Rope & Horses Favourite Treats

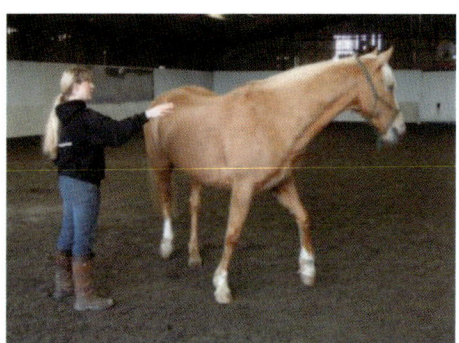

Lesson 1:- After attaching the lead to the head collar, pass it over the withers travelling from near to offside so the end can be held in your left hand whilst you stand at the horse's offside shoulder.

Lesson 2:- Send the horse away from you by applying gentle constant pressure on the neck just behind the jaw with the right hand, whilst telling the horse to go 'Around' or 'Away'. Gradually increase the pressure on the neck until you get a reaction. At the same time keep a constant light tension on the lead, using this only to guide the horse around and away from you in a circle. This action reinforces the pressure aids applied to the neck. The horse should dislike the pressure on his neck enough to yield and follow the light guide of the rope, taking the easier route.

Lesson 3:- On completion of the first full circle, reward your friend well with a friendly rub or scratch on his favourite itchy spot and of course a treat, almost go overboard with verbal praise so the horse can identify that he has done something really good. This will prompt him to think about what it was he just did!

Lesson 4:- Repeat steps 2 & 3 until you hardly have to touch the horse on the neck. If you keep your aids consistent and in a specific order, the horse should start to predict from your body language and vocal cue 'away' that he is due to receive a bit of discomfort in his neck unless he follows the lead and does a nice circle. As your horse moves away from your hand move towards his tail and try to encourage a complete circle with as little guidance as possible on the rope and with a treat at the ready.

Lesson 5:- Once your horse is doing this with virtually no opposition pressure on the neck or rope, you can try removing the rope and head collar and practising loose in the stable. The trick to this is to imagine you still have the guiding rope on the horse and try to emulate the body language you used. The horse will recognise this and follow the invisible guide-line round. Once he does this you have cracked it! Reward him extremely well and practise this daily until perfected. Soon you will be able to just gesture with your hand in the direction you wish the horse to turn whilst saying 'away' and the horse will respond.

Lesson 6:- This should be practised to the left and right rein. To change direction, start by standing at the near side shoulder holding the rope in the right hand and pushing the neck round with the left.

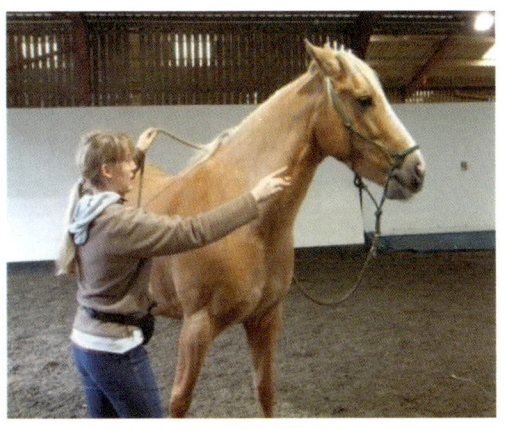
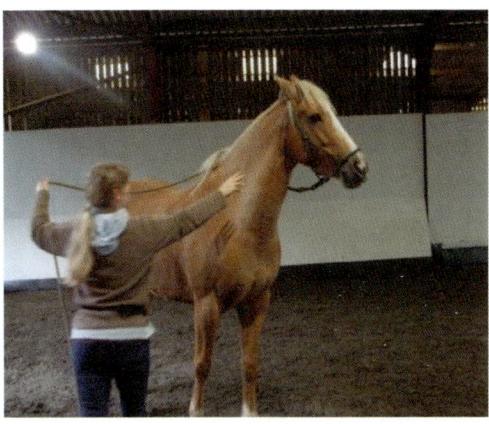
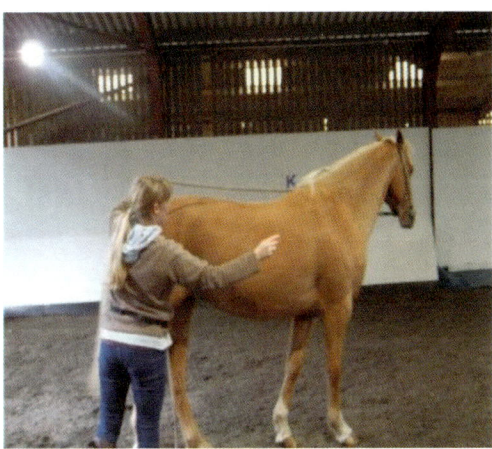
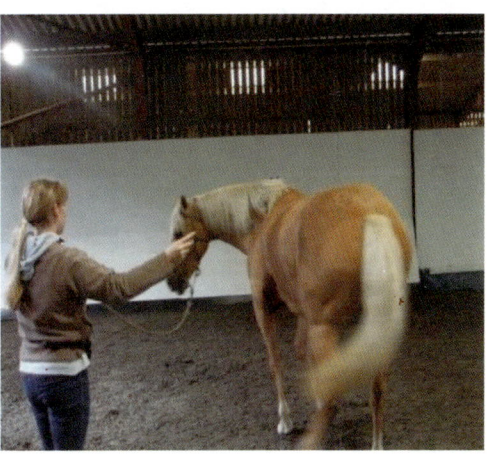

Training Tip: If you reward using food treats, your horse may start to become cheeky on completion of the circle and may try to snatch his expected reward. Therefore it is a good idea to occasionally throw in another command on completion of the circle, such as requesting a step back, lift a front leg, or circle the opposite way.

The Side Pass

52

A perfect and invaluable preparation for the Half Pass; this lesson is also perfect early training to encourage youngsters to yield sideways. The side pass is good practise in manipulating your horse's direction, mastering your self projection, assertive driving abilities and communication.

Tools Required: - Head Collar, Lead Rope, Schooling Whip & Treats

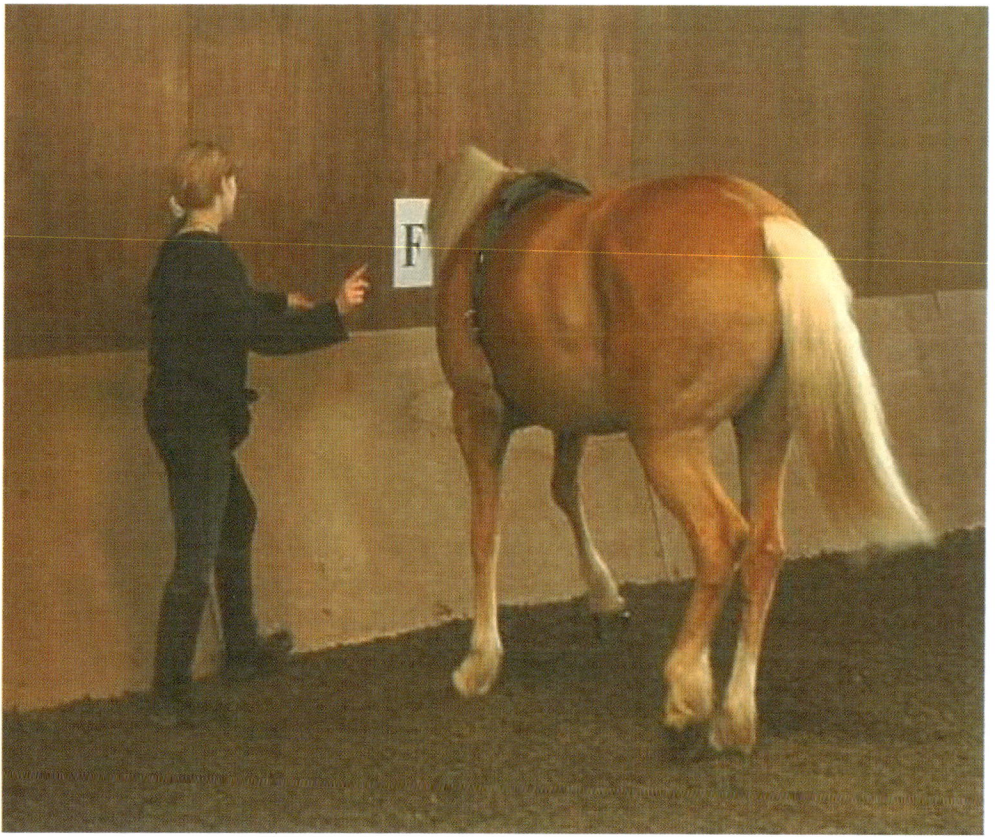

Step 1:- Dress your horse in a head collar and attach a long lead rope. Begin by leading your horse over to face the wall of the school or field fence. Stand to your horse's near-side shoulder with the lead in your left hand and the whip held in the right. Start by asking the horse to 'get over' and begin wiggling the slack rope, lightly at first; slowly increasing in pressure until there is a reaction to move away from you. At the same time lightly push the quarters in the same direction with your whip, again increasing the pressure until the horse makes the slightest effort to move away from you. As soon as there is any try from the horse to do as you ask, stop wiggling the rope and remove the pressure of the whip immediately and reward well. This is so the horse learns that by complying early, they will avoid any discomfort and earn their treat.

Lesson 2:- Repeat stage one until the horse happily offers the movement when faced with the wall and the command to 'get over'. Note as the horse becomes accustomed to the request you should just be able to follow the word cue with the slightest wiggle on the rope and a pointing gesture with the whip towards the quarters.

Lesson 3:- Now you can discard the whip, and practise just wiggling the rope. Should you have trouble with the quarters reinforce your aids by pretending you have an imaginary whip in your hand and use the same body language as you were before. Alternatively if your rope is long enough you should be able to flick the end at your horse's flank to get the same reaction.

Lesson 4:- Next it is time to discard the rope line and attempt it freestyle. Lead you horse over to the wall and remove the rope. You may pick up the whip again in your right hand just to encourage the horse to 'Get over' whilst pretending to wiggle the imaginary 'invisible' rope held in the left hand. Use the whip to reinforce the drive by flicking backwards and forwards between jowl and flank. As soon as you have the slightest try reward well!!!

Lesson 5:- Now completely discard both your lead and whip and replace with your 'invisible' tools and do the same thing and reward as necessary.

Lesson 6:- Once stages 1 to 5 have been successfully completed you can try this without wall support. To do this, revert to using the lead & whip and start the exercise again. Should the horse have any trouble understanding, you may dress him in a bridle and run a supporting guide lunge-line from the horses offside bit ring over the back to be held in the right hand with the right direction. Once the horse understands you will notice little pressure or contact will be needed on the line and it can be discarded and the lesson continued as before.

Training Tip

If your horse has any difficulty in understanding the rope wiggle, reinforce what your are asking by following the wiggle with a gentle push behind the jowl with the whip. Move the whip backwards and forwards between the jowl and the quarters but be careful not to jab with the stick.

Chapter 3: First Steps

54

Now you're ready to get started!

The following chapter starts you with a few simple tricks that test your basic knowledge. They require no elaborate equipment, just your quiet persistence, patience and understanding.

These tricks establish the basics of communication, through consistent body language, position, movement and voice, and you will start to learn how you can use these aids to affect the horse's behaviour and improve his confidence and character.

Take your time, practice little and often, so the horse does not bore of the lessons and keep it fun. If you start to get irritable, stop….. As this will directly be communicated with your horse. Always leave the training on a positive note as this is what your student will remember.

Follow each lesson step in order, and once you have the desired effect, generously reward your horse with loads of love, praise and treats. You will find most of these tricks can be practised in the stable as well as in the field or school; therefore, you can practice them virtually anywhere, anytime when handling your horse. I have found that two short sessions a day generally works best although a great result can be achieved in only one 10 minute session a week.

The tricks in this chapter are suitable for any age horse from yearling upwards. Just by practising them you will end up with a smarter more intelligent horse, and when he figures out there is a bonus prize for each right answer he gives he will be an 'A' grade student always wanting to please his teacher!

These training sessions should be fun and can accompany the horse's normal training program. Keep it fun and enjoyable, the lessons should be light hearted and an event that you both look forward to and enjoy!

Say Cheese!!! The Perfect Smile

This is one of the easiest tricks to start with and has great novelty value. Fantastic as a party trick, it is sure to earn your horse a smile and a laugh from your friends. This will also plant the seeds in your horse's mind of how he can train you to produce that scrumptious treat!

You may have noticed while observing horses that this behaviour occurs naturally. It is widely known as the 'Flehman Response' and is most often caused by a strange smell on the breeze or something touching the horse's nose. Stallions can be seen doing this when one of their mares is in season.

Tools required: - Head-collar, lead-rope, A supply of your horses favourite treats!

Lesson 1:- Dress your horse in head collar and lead rope and tie him up loosely so he will stand still, but make sure he has plenty of room to move his head. Stand to his near side and keep the head steady by holding the lead just below the clip. This first stage is to ensure your horse allows you to handle their head. (If your horse is happy with you touching his face then move directly to stage 2.)

To win your horse's confidence, start by placing a gentle firm hand on his forelock or anywhere that is comfortable and tolerable then slowly rub the area whilst praising him as a good boy. Gradually draw you hand down the face towards the nose, if the horse becomes uncomfortable, retreat back to his comfort zone and tell him he is a good boy. With patience your horse will become comfortable with your hand by this approach and retreat method, by constantly pushing the boundaries of his comfort zone until your horse comfortably accepts the hand all over his head without being head shy or difficult.

Lesson 2:- Now that your horse is fully accepting of you working around and touching his head, you can start the fun part. Stand by the near side shoulder, hold the head steady by holding the lead rein with your left hand just below the clip. Conceal the treat in your right palm and let him sniff your hand. Tell him he is a good boy and reward him for paying attention by giving him the treat.

Lesson 3:- Now that you have your horse's interest, take another treat in the same hand and hold it above the nose. Extend the forefinger on this hand and start to tickle his nose from above whilst asking him to 'smile'. As you get closer to the sensitive area between the nostrils heading for the top lip you should get a reaction from your horse by him starting to curl his top lip and raise his head. As soon as there is the slightest try (even the smallest quiver of the lip!) cease tickling and reward him immediately with the treat and buckets of praise!!!

Lesson 4:- Keep your training sessions brief so the horse will not tire of the game, but continue to repeat steps 2 and 3 until you horse learns to predict that when you ask for a 'smile' and point at his nose he will give you his biggest, cheekiest grin ever! This trick can be practised anywhere, so you can practise anytime you handle your horse.

Very soon you will just be able to say 'smile' to get a glimpse of those pearly whites. Do the trick methodically so your horse will learn to pre-empt what you want him to do. For instance, say 'Smile', just as you start to reach to tickle him on the nose, eventually he will learn that the word cue 'smile' precedes the tickles and will smile on the cue word to avoid a tickled nose, speeding up the arrival of his award for obliging.

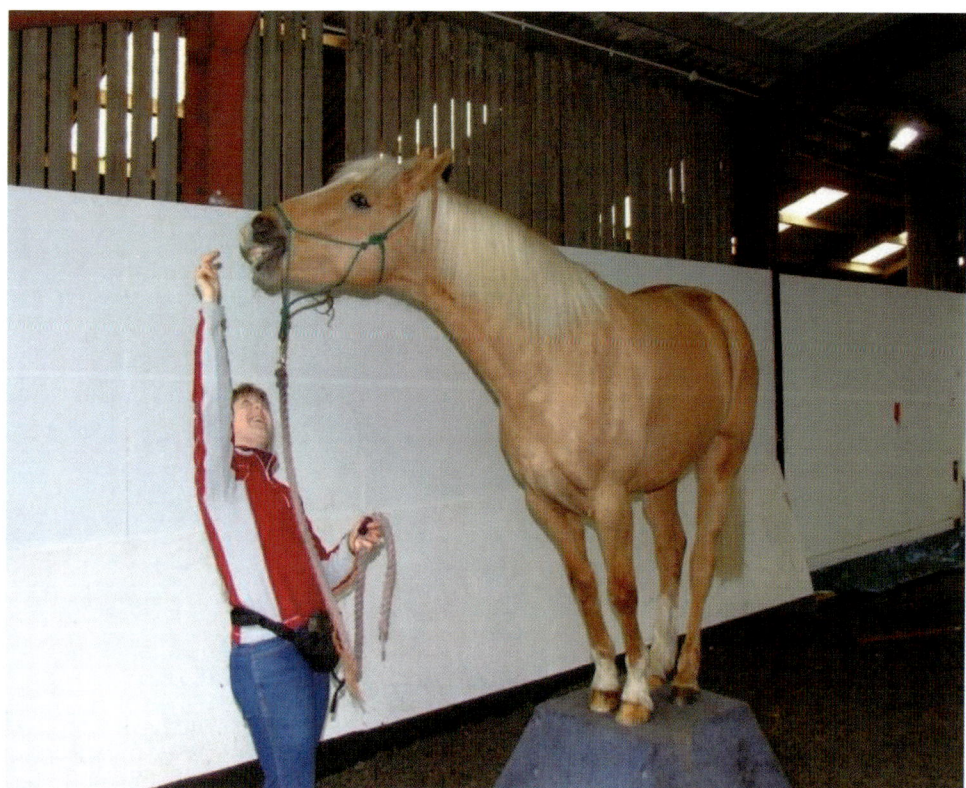

Give Us a Big Sloppy Kiss!

How about a big sloppy smooch to show how much you care!

You will be teaching your horse how to touch something on cue with his nose, in this case your face, so he will earn a reward. You will see the bulb flick on between your horse's ears when he suddenly figures out the point of the lesson. Just remember to steer clear of the garlic feed & prepare to be smothered in horsey smooches!

Tools required: - Head Collar, Lead Rope & Supply of horse favourite treat-Suggest Breath Mints!

Lesson 1:- Dress your horse in a head collar with lead rope and tie him up so he will stand still. Standing in front of him, conceal a treat in your fist, and let him sniff the back of your hand so he knows it's there. As soon as he touches your hand with his nose, give him the treat and tell him he is good.

Lesson 2:- Tilting your head back slightly, conceal another treat in your hand, let him sniff the hand again to know it's there and then raise your closed hand up to your cheek. With the same hand use the index finger to point at your cheek and ask for a 'Kiss'.

Lesson 3:- Repeat stage two until the horse is naturally following your hand and happily nuzzling it for the treat whilst you point at your cheek requesting a 'kiss'. Start now withholding the treat until the horse accidentally touches you on the cheek next to your finger, as soon as there is the slightest contact with your cheek, reward him. This stage may take several lessons for the horse to associate the touch of the cheek with the opening of your hand for the reward.

Lesson 4:- Once the horse is happily doing what you ask and nuzzling you on the cheek, repeat the exercise gesturing towards your face with your hand. Remember to continue tilting your head back as this will be the final prompting body language. If the horse follows the hand point again at the cheek but do not reward him until there is contact with your cheek again. Repeat until just by tilting your head back and asking for a 'Kiss' you horse happily begins nuzzling your cheek.

Lesson 5:- Once the horse is happily nuzzling you on the cheek, you should be reasonable confident he will not nip you. So if you are brave enough you can ask for the big slobber on the lips from your Casanova! Just make sure your horse has not been on the Garlic!

Important** Reasonable care must be taken as horse can nip or bite whether intentionally or by accident, so teach this trick cautiously at your own risk.

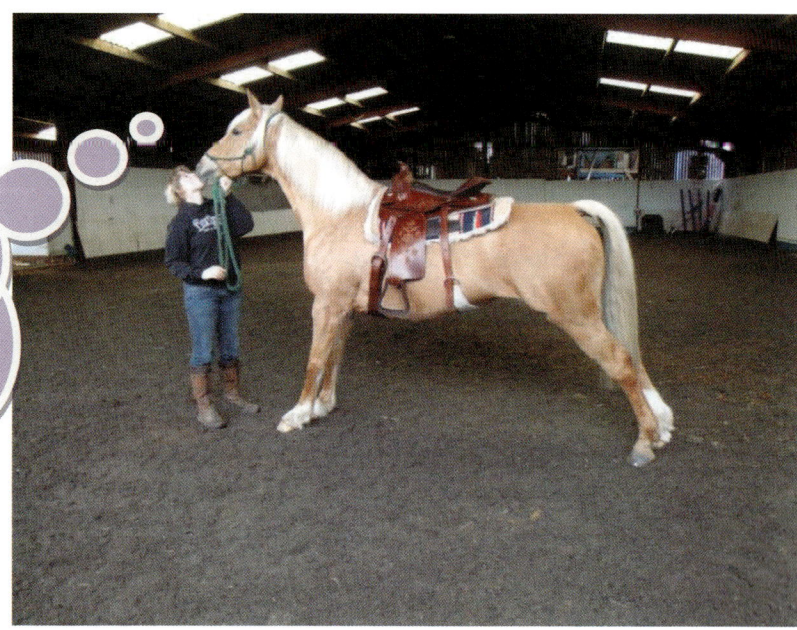

Love you! Love your carrots!

How About a Hug Then?

Teach your horse to show you how much he cares by learning to give you a cuddle! Combine this with the 'Kiss Me' trick to show your friends what a little Romeo your horse can be. Just don't forget the bouquet of carrots on his or her birthday!

Tools Required: Head Collar, Lead Rope, Treats, Clicker

Lesson 1: Dress your horse in the head collar and lead rope and stand in a quiet and familiar area so your horse can concentrate on his lesson. Your horse's own stable is ideal for this. Don't tie your horse up as he will need freedom to move his head as required. Position yourself at your horse's near side shoulder facing in the same direction as him holding the lead rope in the left hand and a treat in your right.

Ask 'Can I have a hug?' (Repeating throughout the lesson, emphasising the word HUG), and hold the treat close over your right shoulder. As your horse reaches for the treat, give a gentle pull on the lead rope making your horse's chin touch your shoulder. As soon as the chin touches your shoulder, release the rope pressure, acknowledge immediately with the clicker, reward with the treat and make a loving fuss of your friend.

Lesson 2: Repeat lesson 1 until your horse recognises by touching your shoulder with his chin he gets rewarded. He should react to the verbal cue accompanied by you tapping your shoulder and you are aiming for your horse to relax and rest his head there until you produce the click and treat.

Lesson 3: Once your horse likes resting his chin on your shoulder, start placing the treat in your left hand. Ask for the chin on the shoulder and then show the treat in your left hand, ask your horse to follow the treat as you drop your hand to your side whilst again asking for a 'HUG', this encourages the horse to curl his head and neck around you giving the appearance of the affectionate hug. Click, treat and praise well at the slightest try in the right direction.

Oh so Shy!

If your goal is to one day give trick performances with your four legged friend, you will undoubtedly know that things do not always go to plan when working with animals and mistakes can be made.

You job is to make your horse look good even if he makes a mistake and this trick could be the answer. Your horse will look even smarter when he looks shy, easily embarrassed or ashamed over a mistake or comical telling off routine, and this will endear him even more to his public!

Tools Required: Head Collar, Lead Rope, Treats, Clicker

Lesson 1: With your horse dressed in a head collar and lead rope stand him in a quiet area such as his own stable so he can relax and concentrate on his lesson. Position yourself in front of your horse. Hold a treat in your left hand behind you in the small of your back, and raise your right arm holding the clicker.

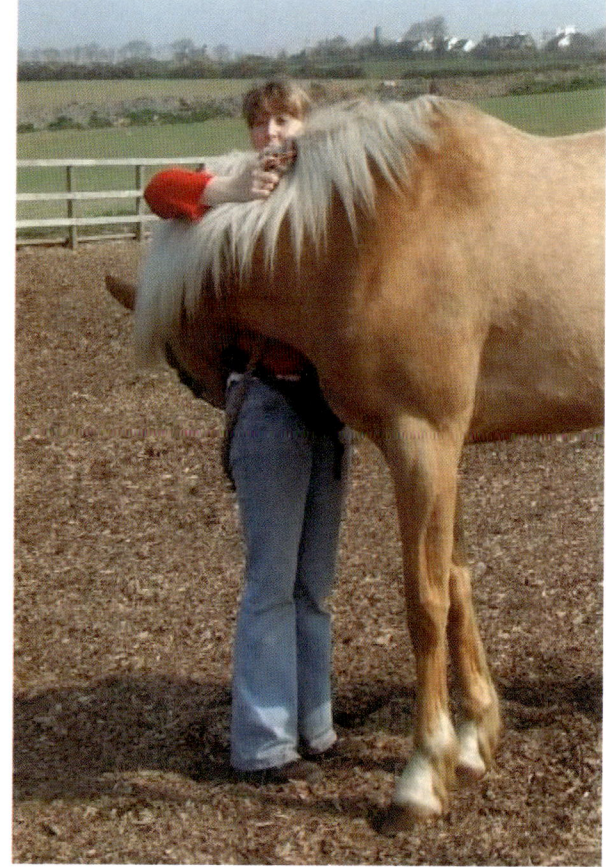

Twist slightly to show your horse the treat is there and give a verbal cue like 'Ahhh he's shy!'. Keep enticing him to drop his head under your arm for the treat and repeating the verbal cues until he is in the right position to pretend he is shy or hiding in shame. As soon as the head is in the correct position, click and reward well, make a big fuss telling him he has done well. Keep the lessons short, roughly five minutes a time so your horse does not get bored with the game and lose interest.

Lesson 2: - Repeat lesson one lengthening the period he spends in this position and as he gets better you can slowly drop your right arm to pet his head.

Right: Oh hide me Mum! I'm too shy!

Yes & No

The Yes & No tricks are achieved through cueing another of the horses natural behaviours. By imitating an annoying fly we can trigger the shake reflex in the horse's neck to imitate a 'Yes' or 'No' response as required.

A lot of comical fun can be had asking your horse questions to which the horse can respond with a Yes or No. Your little clown will have the audience rolling in the aisles with laughter!

Tools Required: Head Collar, Lead Rope, Treats, Blunt Nail, Clicker & Schooling Whip

CARE* PLEASE take great care when using the nail in the following instructions. You are trying to imitate the irritation of something as light as a fly on your horse coat and as such only the lightest touch of the nail is needed, take care not to prick or jab your horse as you will break the skin and end up with a sore horse and probably a bite or two yourself.

Lesson 1: Let's begin with the nod for 'Yes'. Dress your horse in head collar and lead rope and tie him up with plenty of slack so he can move his head freely. Next, stand at your horses left shoulder facing towards your horses head. With the nail in your left hand, very gently touch your horse on the chest between the front legs. The reaction you are looking for is the horse to bob his head to bite at the annoying sensation he is feeling on his chest, like he is trying to scare off a fly or stinging insect. At the slightest downward nod click and reward well. It is likely you will need to experiment with finding the exact place to touch to get the best reaction from your horse. Horses vary in their sensitivity and therefore vary in their ticklish spots. If you get absolutely no reaction from the chest, less sensitive creatures often respond to gently touching under the chin. Keep the training session short, finish after the first or second correct reaction in each lesson and put him out to play and think about the lessons.

Lesson 2: Repeat lesson 1 until the horse is comfortably nodding his head. At this stage you can try and discard the nail and replace it with a light tap with the end of your whip. Repeat and reward until the horse is comfortably giving the same reaction. If the horse ignores the whip follow it up with the nail and clicker. The horse will soon learn the light tap of the whip precedes the touch of the nail and will begin to react to the whip when asked.

Lesson 3: Keep practising lesson 2 until you only need to gesture without touching to the same point on the chest with the whip to get the same reaction. Reward well and leave the lesson as soon as he has done as requested two or three times.

Lesson 4: Now think up a couple of questions your horse can answer 'Yes' to. Your horse will learn the light tap of the whip precedes the touch of the nail and will begin to react to the whip when asked.

Lesson 5: So what if the answer in 'No'! To encourage the horse to give the 'No' reflex you need to provoke the sideways shake of the head. In this case, go back to lesson one and repeat the lesson sequence, but this time you are applying the touch of the nail to the horse neck around the wither region. When you get the slightest shake click and reward well, follow the same sequence, replacing nail with the whip etc. Again you may have to experiment with finding your horses most sensitive area, the less sensitive horse often reacts better to the touch further up the neck or just behind the ear.

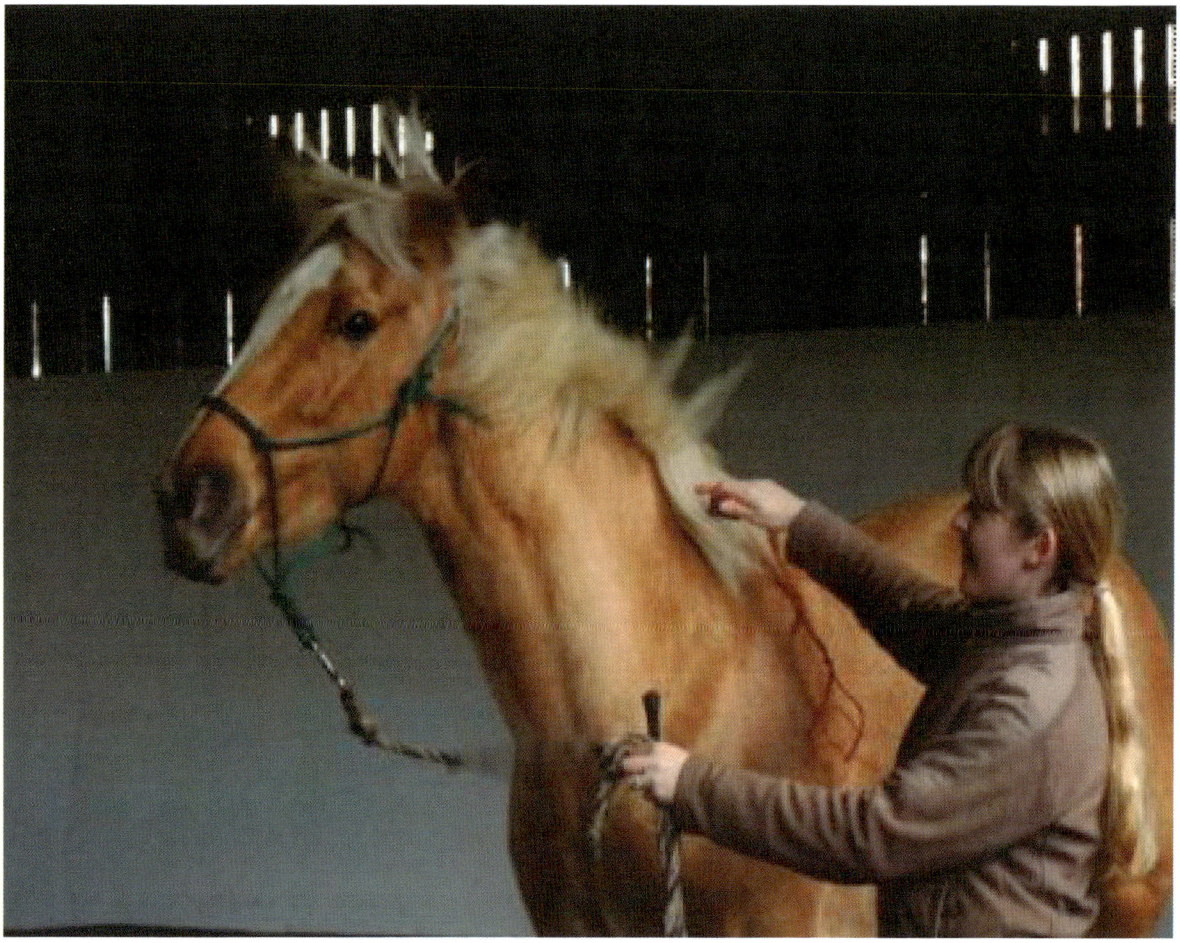

Give Us a Push!

Your horse will love this trick. It's not often your horse is allowed to push you around so he will absolutely relish the opportunity to have fun with this one. The best time for this is when your horse has not had attention for some time and is waiting for his tea or breakfast when he is feeling a little bit cheeky!

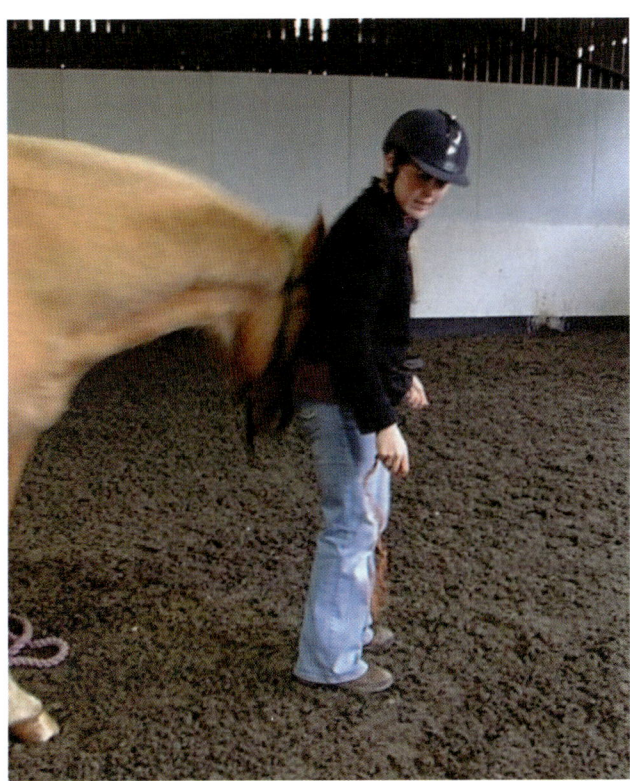

However please be warned, unless you are very strict about rewarding your horse for performing this only when asked, this trick can become a nuisance behaviour. I recommend that it is used only by experienced trainers, or those who specifically want to use it as part of comical routine.

Tools Required: Head Collar, Lead Rope, Treats, Clicker

Lesson 1: Holding your horse's favourite treat in your hand, show it to him to grab his attention and then conceal it teasingly so he starts to sniff and hunt for it. With your horse sniffing your hand hold it to your lower back encouraging him to drop his head. As he follows your hand, keep your hand closed and lean gently backwards against his face repeating the verbal cue 'PUSH'. Your horses naturally response will be a resistance reflex and will probably give you a nudge to tell you to get off whilst he pursues the treat. As soon as you feel the slightest nudge, click, reward and praise your four legged friend.

Lesson 2: Repeat the first lesson, leaning a little heavier on your horse, repeating the word cue 'PUSH', and continuing to reward again for the slightest resistance in his hunt for the treat. Keep repeating until the horse starts putting some effort into the nudge. You'll find that this should not take long as your horse's natural cheekiness will enjoy the opportunity to playfully push you around.

Lesson 3: Repeat the training until you get a good push in reaction to turning your back on your horse and giving the verbal cue 'Push'. Click and treat on each correct response. You'll soon have to watch your back or you may get a cheeky push when you least expect it, this is ideal for trick performances, but if you don't want your horse to push until you verbally ask, don't treat unless you have asked for the behaviour first.

Left & Right Please!

Now it's time to get your horse really thinking! The beauty of this trick is the horse has the choice of several answers. It is only through watching you carefully and listening to your word cues your horse will be able to answer correctly and win his prize! Your friends and any on lookers will be amazed when you horse shows he knows his left from his right. Alternatively the same cue may be used to say 'Please!'

Later in the book you will see how this same trick will evolve into the elegant Spanish Walk and Trot, and why it is so important your horse understands you when you request a particular leg to be lifted on cue.

Tools Required: - Head Collar, Lead Rope, and Treats & Schooling Whip.

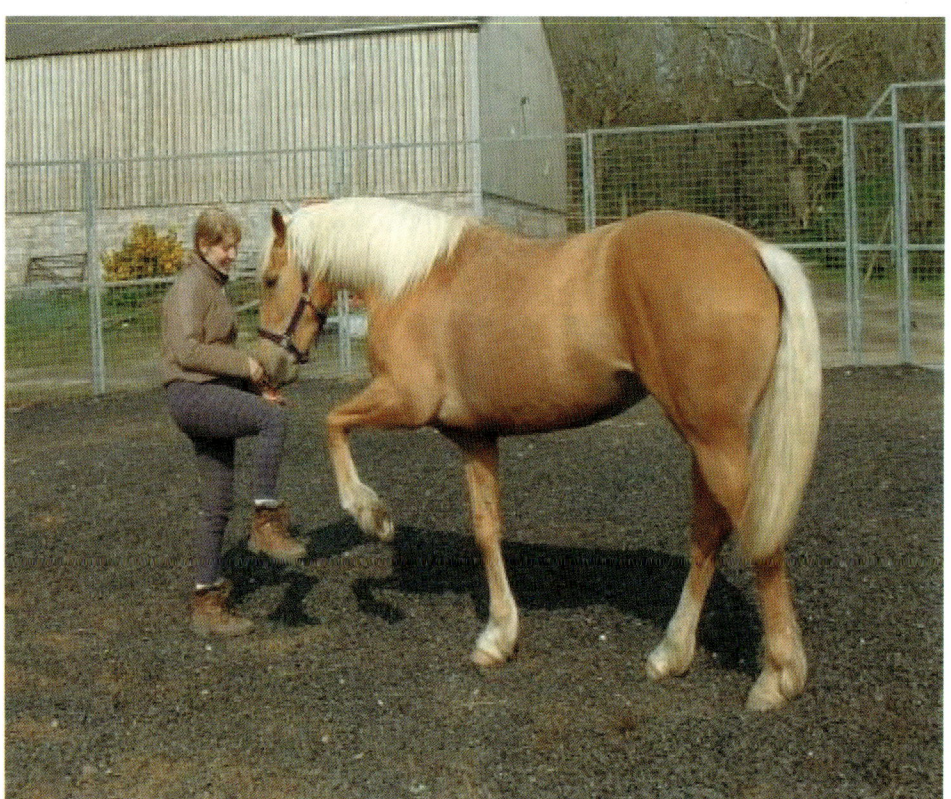

Lesson 1:- Dress your horse in head collar and lead rope and tie him up securely. Stand at your horse's left shoulder and gently tap his left pastern with the schooling whip whilst saying the word 'left please'. As soon as there is any reaction in the leg, reward the horse and praise him well, even if it is just a twitch or a move of the leg backwards! Practice this until you only have to gesture towards the leg with the whip and the leg is lifted on the voice cue 'Left please!'

It can also help if you stand in front of him or to the side and lift the same leg as a guide for the horse.

Lesson 2:- To get your horse to cue 'right', reverse the above instructions by standing at his right shoulder and tapping the right pastern with the schooling whip. Repeat as in stage one until the horse reacts to the voice cue 'right'.

Lesson 3:- Start to alternate the requests for 'right' or 'left' leg. You will see your horse thinking about what you're saying. If you decide he needs a prompt, gesture to the appropriate leg with the whip and re-emphasize the cue. Always ensure as soon as the horse offers the correct leg your reward him well.

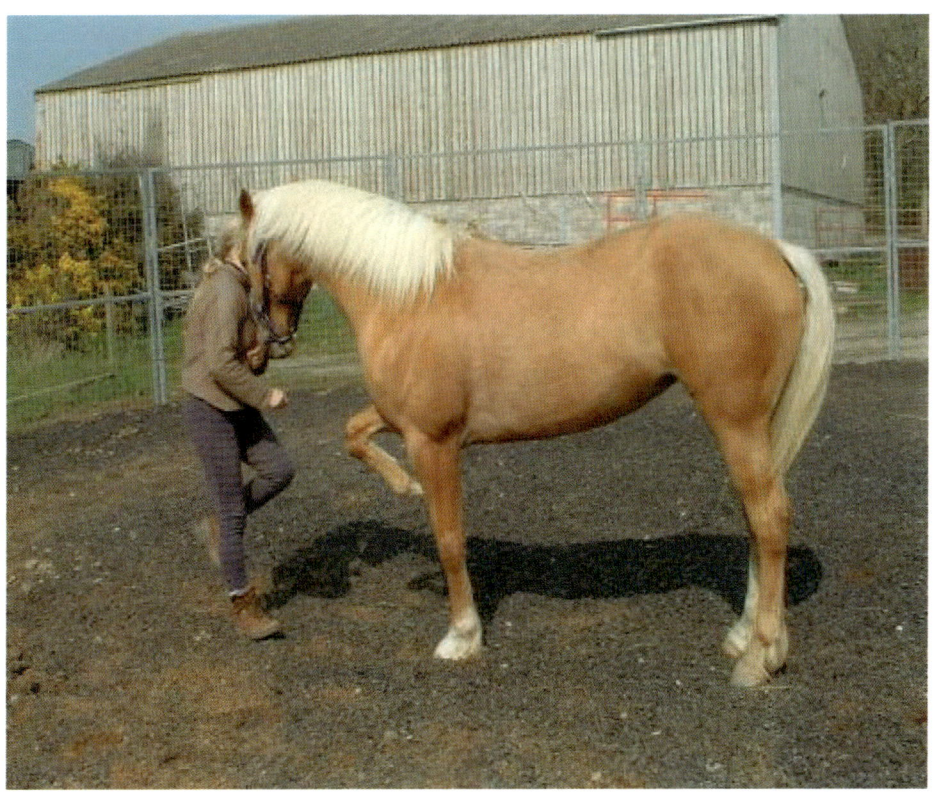

Lesson 4:- Keep practising until your horse can differentiate between both cues. You can retain your secret hints by standing in front of your horse and shifting your weight from one leg to the other very subtly so he can follow your body language. Practise little and often every time your horse is handled, with plenty of praise.

Let's Shake On It!

Horses often offer a foreleg without being asked for it, they paw the ground to beg for food or attention. This is the behaviour we wish to prompt on cue, so the horse will offer you a foreleg wishing to politely shake hands or hooves!

Take care you do not reward the horse for the following behaviour unless you have requested it. Doing so can lead to dangerous striking with the front leg when least expected.

Tools Required: Head Collar, Lead Rope, Long Soft (12ft) Lead Rope, Whip, Treats, and Clicker

Lesson 1:- Dressed in head collar and lead rope tie your horse up loosely in a quiet and familiar area such as the stable. Decide which hoof you want him to 'shake hands' with, if you know your horse well you can probably tell if he is right or left hooved by which he usually strikes off with in canter. Make a note of this next time you ride, as your he will probably be happier offering the same leg to shake hands with. Next, gently loop the snap end of the long soft lead around the pastern of the leg. Reassure your horse that everything is okay and spend a little time familiarising him with having the rope around his leg. Tell him he is good and reward to help him relax.

Once he appears comfortable, gently raise the hoof forward and upwards by pulling up on the rope whilst saying the verbal cue 'Shake' and offering your spare hand to shake. Keep practising until your horse will raise the leg to the horizontal with hardly any prompting through the rope and your can take hold of the hoof. Click, reward and praise for every effort in the right direction.

Lesson 2: Next remove the rope and repeat. Offer your hand and ask for a 'Shake'. Even if the hoof doesn't lift all the way, click and reward well and lift the hoof higher with your spare hand. Gently shake whilst praising. Repeat until your horse enthusiastically offers the leg on cue.

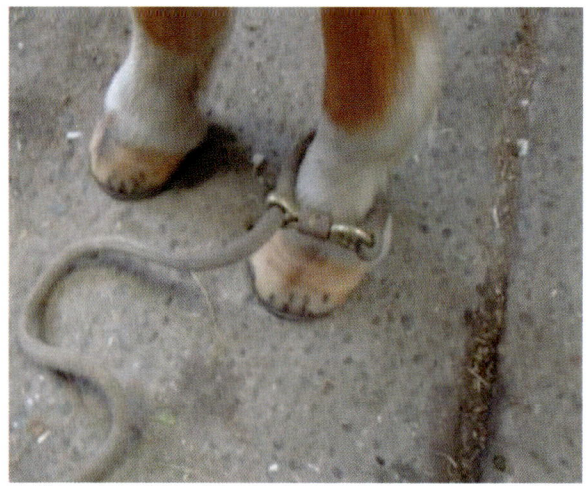

What's 1 + 1 =?

How on earth can a horse learn to count? Your horse can appear to be an absolute genius and you can stun your friends or any audience with this mystifying trick. You can have great fun, asking your horse to add, subtract, count out ages, solve mathematical riddles, and tell the time, the only limit here is your imagination or personal math abilities.

Tools Required: - Head Collar, Lead Rope, and Schooling Whip & Treats

Lesson 1:- Dressed in head collar and lead rope tie your horse up loosely. Position yourself at your horse's near side shoulder facing forwards. Take the whip and begin to gently tap your horses near fore pastern whilst asking him to 'Count'. As soon as there is a reaction and the horse stomps with the hoof, immediately cease the whip contact whilst clicking, treating and praising well. Keep the training sessions short, approximately 10 minutes a lesson should suffice.

Lesson 2:- Keep practising lesson 1 until the horse gives a stomping action every time you tap the foot. As your horse gets the hang of this, ask for several stomps before rewarding. This is easier if you count out loud and aim for a target number each time.

Lesson 3:- Repeat the lessons, asking your horse specific questions, such as what is 2 + 3? Tap his foot so that he raises it 5 times and to ensure he stops when you want him to all you need to do is to take a step forward. Moving in front of the horse shoulder is a blocking movement that communicates the horse should stop.

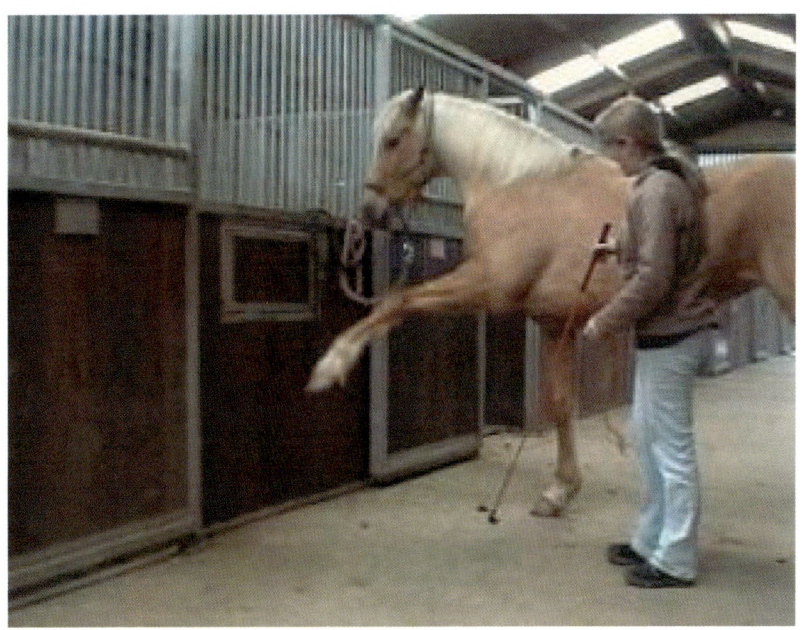

The Stretch!

This is a regal and showy way to present your horse in the show ring. The position is often seen naturally in elegant breeds like the Saddle bred or Arabian. It is also a great way of practising how to manipulate your horse's posture and teach him patience whilst holding a pose for you.

As a practical stretching technique, it is a great exercise for conditioning and to help build a strong back. Take care now to introduce this slowly and not to hold the pose for too long in the initial stages to avoid straining or injuring weak or unfit animals.

Some trainers also use this as an easier way to mount their horse as the stronger the horse gets the further the stretch and thus the stirrup hangs a lot lower making it easier to reach. I must emphasise that mounting this way is not a good idea unless you have a very fit animal, otherwise it puts a lot of stress on your horse's poor back and could cause injury.

Tools required: Head Collar, Lead rope, Treats, Clicker, and Schooling Whip

What a show off! Let's pose for the camera! Fern is modelling her stylish winter woollies.

Lesson 1: Dress your horse in head collar and lead rope. Fill a pocket with treats. Stand him next to a wall or fence to restrict unwanted movement and position yourself at your horse's near side shoulder facing towards the tail. Take the lead rope in your left hand just below the lead clip to hold the head steady, and hold the clicker box in your right hand. Stand your horse up square and ask your horse to hold this position as long as possible. Refresh yourself and your horse with 'standing still and correct' exercise (page 47), click and reward when completed satisfactorily.

Lesson 2: Once your horse is standing correctly, ensure that the head is raised with the chin held high… Ask the horse to 'stay' and hold the position until you use the clicker, reward well. If the horse moves before you click, say no and reposition correctly before continuing this exercise. Keep the periods short before rewarding. Repeat the exercise, gradually increasing the length of time your horse holds the pose.

Lesson 3: Next comes the stretching! With your horse successfully holding the position detailed above, ask for the near front leg to be lifted whilst repetitively asking the horse to 'Stretch'. Gently take the leg by the fetlock and pull the leg forward a couple of inches, ask the horse to place the foot on the floor in this position., if the horse complies follow it up with a verbal 'stay' and try and hold the same position for a few seconds before clicking and rewarding well. Most horses will not comply straight away; they will try and snatch the leg back. If they do this successfully then you are holding the leg too tight. Cup the fetlock joint in your hand and gently guide it forward, do not try and grab the leg as the horse's natural instinct is to pull, fight and back away. Any improvement to the forward position of the leg must be praised and rewarded well… Continue to practise the length of time your horse holds each position. Clicking and treating.

Lesson 4: Repeat lesson 3, for 5 minutes a day until your horse understands and can be positioned fairly quickly. Reward and go overboard with the praise every time your horse holds the position. Delay the click a little longer on each occasion asking for the pose to be held for a few more seconds on each try. Your horse will begin to understand that once they hear that click they have finished and done well, so they will listen out and do their best to hold their pose until they hear you use the clicker box.

Training Tip: Sometimes your horse won't put his front feet down where you want him to, but will try and snatch his foot back or will waive it in the air. If this happens you need to ask him to shift his weight so he has to put the hoof down when asked to. If it is the front right leg then place his toe and then gently pull his head to the right and vice versa with the left leg.

End of Trail Pose

This is another challenge in moulding your horse's pose into a desired position. The 'End of Trail' pose is also useful for stretching the top line and improving balance. Practised early it can be a good preparation for Piaffe and pedestal work whilst benefiting dressage divas as a collecting exercise. Horses with weak backs or quarters will also find this is an ideal strengthening exercise.

Tools Required: Head Collar, Lead Rope, Treat, Clicker, Schooling Whip

Lesson 1: Dress your horse in his head collar, lead rope and stand him up nice and square and ask him to 'Stay'. Request your horse holds this position and after a few seconds click, treat and reward well.

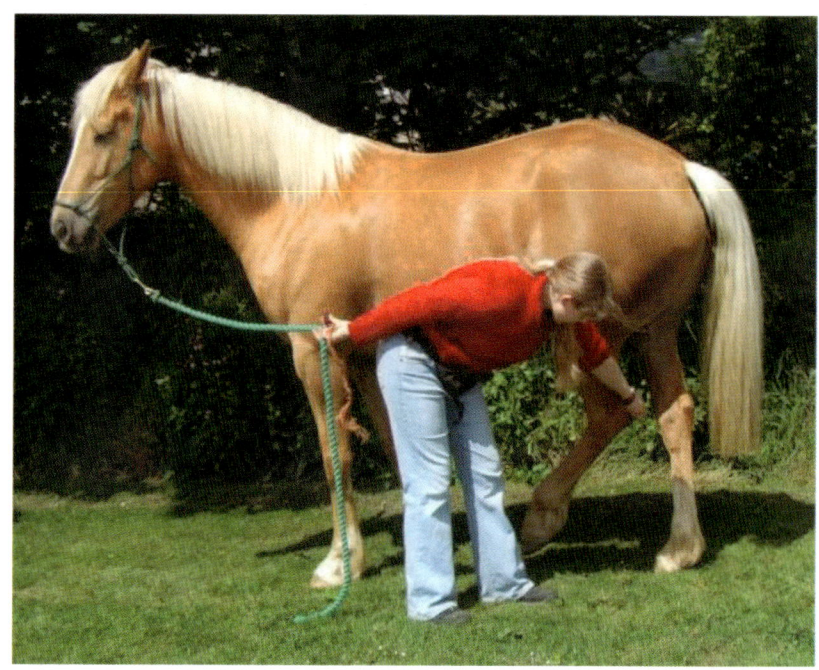

Lesson 2: Next with your horse standing square next to a fence or a wall to prevent unwanted movement, position yourself at your horses left shoulder holding the lead rein in your left and the schooling whip in your right. Now gently ask your horse to position his head forwards and downwards. Ask for him to hold the position again and treat and reward.

Lesson 3: Ask your horse to adopt the square leg position and drop his head again as in lesson 2. Insist your horse stays and whilst still holding the rope to discourage any forward movement, position yourself close to your horse's flank. If you horse moves at all, correct him and stand him up correctly before continuing. Gently run your hand over your horse's rump and down the back legs whilst gently reminding him to stay. Repeat until you can do this for at least 60 seconds and then return to your horse's nose before clicking, rewarding and praising him well.

Lesson 4: Now position you and your horse as previously practised in lesson 3 so you are standing at your horse's quarters. Run your hand down your horse's near side leg until you reach the point of hock. Now remind your horse to 'stay'. Gently start to squeeze the skin over the point of hock between thumb and index finger.

Ensure you squeeze gently and don't pinch, squeeze just hard enough for your horse to pick up his leg, as soon as he does push the back of his leg to make him step forward with it as he places it back on the floor. Reward well for the slightest try in the right direction. If your horse moves his front feet, stop immediately and correct him, so he stands square again before repeating the cue on the hind leg.

Lesson 5: Repeat lesson 4 but standing in the same position next to your horse, practice the pinch and lift forward on the offside hoof. Repeat with alternating legs to encourage them slowly and gradually forward underneath your horse's body. Clicking and rewarding for every correct step. Keep practising this on a daily basis and always insist your horse keeps his front feet absolutely still.

Lesson 6: With practise you will be able to gesture toward the hocks with your hand or crop to get your horse to step underneath with both back legs. Eventually your horse will be able to place the hind feet about 8 to 10 inches from the front feet and hold the pose. Later you will see how the time you have invested in this task will benefit you and your horse in pedestal work and collecting work, such as Piaffe.

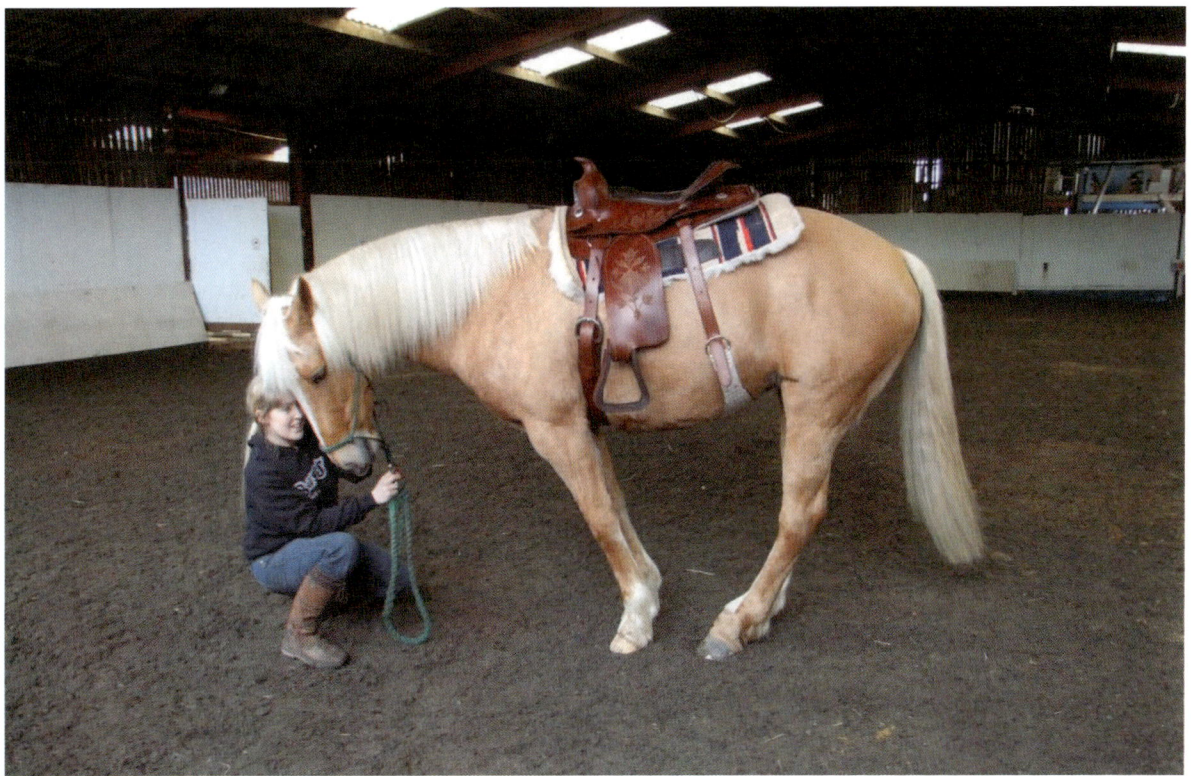

Above: *The end of trail pose is fantastic for stretching the top line and practising communication!*

Chapter 4: Introducing Props

A lot of fun can be had familiarising your horse with new and unusual items. Your horse will soon get over his fears and enjoy playing with and investigating his new toys. Using props will make the lessons more interesting and will get him thinking and using his reasoning powers to work out exactly what is being asked of him.

Once the horse is familiar with using props, anything new and unusual is potentially a new toy. He will learn to trust you when you ask him to investigate or face new things in the same casual manner. Realising it can be a fun game, he will soon learn, you his friend, would never ask him to do anything that would hurt him. Your horse's confidence and inquisitive nature will shine through.

Use your imagination and have fun. Anything is possible! Fern particularly enjoyed being introduced to a paint brush and blank canvas. Who knows, she could be the first horse to exhibit in the Tate Modern!

Take care though when choosing props as they must be safe for your horse to handle and up to rough treatment. As with toys for young children, your horse will chew on or put things in his mouth. You must ensure there are no small parts to swallow, dangerous sharp edges, flimsy parts or toxic contents, like flaky paint or poisonous liquids in bottles. If in doubt don't use it, there are plenty of other toys out there and you can't go far wrong if you use similar props to the ones used in the following pages.

Hold a Target Object

73

Horses are naturally inquisitive creatures and given the chance will investigate strange items or situations. To do this they will use their extremely flexible muzzles, lips and sensitive whiskers to explore the world around them.

Using this natural curiosity, we can show a horse how to manipulate other objects. For example, to collect and retrieve their feeding bowl, to close and open doors, to pickup and handle unusual objects such as waving a flag, holding a drinking bottle, picking up blankets etc, teaching your horse to paint. Think outside the box! This trick is limited only by your imagination.

Tools required: - Head collar, Lead Rope, Treats, and a safe object of choice.

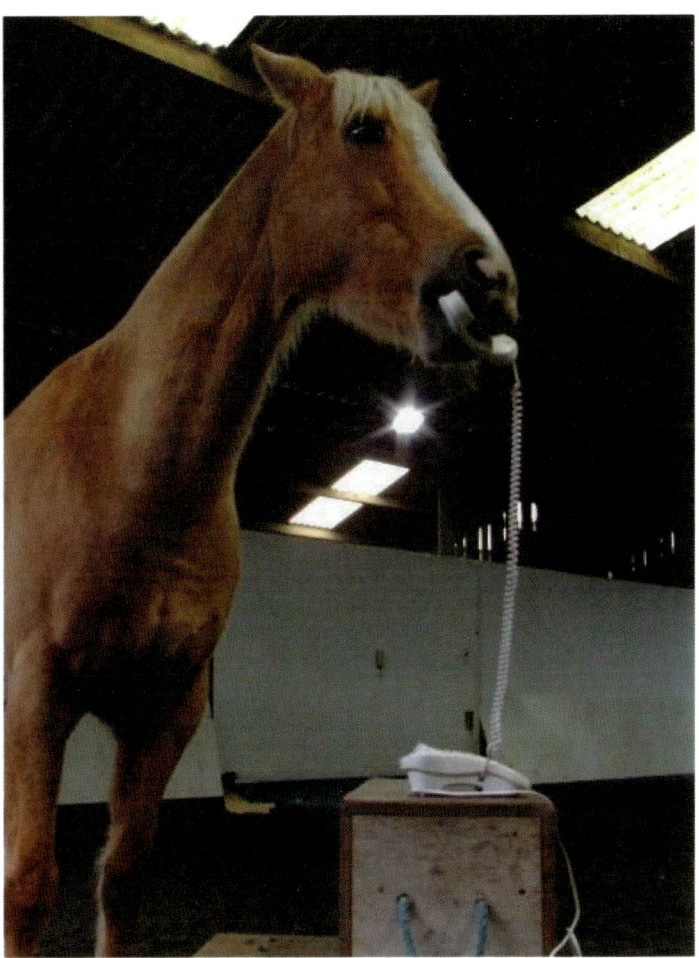

Lesson 1:- Start by tying up your horse in his stable or to a fence dressed in his head collar. Hold your selected item under your horse's muzzle and say 'hold'. As soon as there is the slightest try to sniff or touch the object, reward with a treat and praise him well.

Lesson 2:- As you horse becomes accustomed to mouthing the object start with-holding the treat until the horse tries to take hold of the object by the mouth or teeth. Keep repeating the verbal cue 'Hold'.

Lesson 3:- Keep practising Step 2 until the horse clearly associates taking the object in the mouth with the end reward and offers the correct action. Vary the item you wish the horse to take to keep your horse's interest!

Left: It's for you Mum! Shall I take a message!

Toot Your Own Horn!

74

An unusual trick that is not only fun and entertaining, but also builds on your horse's confidence by desensitising the horse to unusual noises to the extent that he will begin to enjoy making the noise himself for reward! This is also an interesting way of teaching your horse to ask for his dinner and a big hit if your aim is to perform for an audience one day!

Fern takes great pleasure in letting me know it is dinner time by honking her horn! I have been known to fasten it to her stable door for her to play, much to the alarm of startled passers by. The nature of your horse will determine how long he takes to adapt to the new toy. A laid back horse may take to this straight away, but some patience and time may need to be spent working with a nervous individual.

Tools Required: Head Collar, Lead Rope, Old Fashioned Bicycle Horn, Treats, and clicker

Above: *A clever horse will learn to toot his own horn*

Lesson 1: You must first accustom your horse to his new noisy toy. Before every meal bring your horse into the stable and prepare the dinner in front of him so they anticipate a good feed. Once you have your horse's attention with the expectation of food, start to honk the horn whilst you are outside of the stable. Follow this up immediately with his nice dinner.

Ensure you start from a distance so your horse does not jump out of his skin. As the minutes or days go by you should be able to get closer and closer whilst making the noise. The purpose is to get your horse to link the idea of something pleasant like his dinner or breakfast with this new noise.

Lesson 2: When your horse appears completely at ease with the noise. Dress him in his head collar and lead rope and tie him up in his stable or yard where he feels comfortable with no distractions. Stand in front of your horse and hold the horn out for your horse to sniff and investigate. As soon as your horse touches the bulb of the horn with his nose click, reward and praise him well. Repeat this several times until he recognises touching the horn gets him a pressie!

Lesson 3: Start by refreshing your horse with lesson 2. Next squeeze on the horn to give a little honk and hold it out so your horse may touch it with his nose again, Repeat the click, reward and praise on each occasion.

Lesson 4: Once your horse obviously associates touching the horn for a reward, offer it to him again but this time do not reward for just touching it. Keep holding it out and offering it to him, when he realises the reward is not forthcoming he will keep trying to make his attempt more obvious to prompt a reward from you and will start mouthing and may even try and bite the bulb. Be careful though, you need to hold the bulb so you can honk it yourself should he attempt to mouth or nuzzle it and not lose a finger in the process. This will make the horse think he honked the horn. Click, reward and praise for any attempt to take the bulb in his mouth.

Lesson 5: Keep asking your horse to take the bulb of the horn in his mouth but as your horse get better, withhold the reward so the horse tries harder to get your attention by biting the horn harder. As soon as there is a good attempt to honk the horn, reward and go overboard with the praise and excitement. Your enthusiasm will rub off on your horse and he will try and repeat what he did to please you.

Lesson 6: Keep practising lesson 5 and your horse will soon take any opportunity to honk the horn for his treat, breakfast or dinner. Whilst teaching this trick you can ask 'Honk if Your Hungry' before presenting the horn to your horse. Your four-legged pal will soon associate this with the trick and the food rewards, and will happily honk away until the food arrives. It is also interesting at this stage to place the horn in the stable or on the field post so you horse can remind you when dinner is running late!

Can I Take Your Hat Ma'am?

In this trick your horse can act as the perfect host by learning to politely take your hat, hold it for you and return it to you when you ask for it. For this you will need to purchase or dig out an old hat from your wardrobe. A hat made of soft flexible material that you have worn will retain your scent and be recognised by your horse, it will also be easy and comfortable for the horse to pick up in his teeth.

Tools Required: Head Collar, Lead Rope, Old Hat (with a high crown or rim your horse will be able to grip), Treats, and Clicker.

Lesson 1: Dressed in head collar and lead rope tie your horse up with plenty of slack so he can move his head freely. Stand in front of your horse and show him the hat in your hand. Place a few treats on the rim, peak, or crown, and allow him to take the treats from the hat. Repeat a few times while telling him what a good boy he is.

Lesson 2: Repeat step one but ask your horse to 'Hold' or 'Take the hat', until your horse tries to nuzzle or take the hat in his teeth. As soon as there is the slightest try, click and reward. Keep practising this lesson until your horse is happily taking the hat when asked. If the hat is dropped, tell your horse off with a verbal 'No', and start from the beginning, never reward for dropping the hat. Always try and ask for the hat back before a drop so your horse gets used to returning it to you for his reward.

Lesson 3: Next step is to ask your horse to take the hat from your head. Tip your head towards him and ask him to take the hat, click and reward on the slightest try. It should only take a couple of seconds before he twigs he has to take the hat from your head. As soon as the hat is removed, ask him to 'hold' for a second and then ask for it back before click, praise and rewarding him.

Lesson 4: Rehearse lesson 3 until your horse masters the removal and return of your hat. Now you are going to ask your horse to retrieve your hat. Ensure your horse is untied and can move his head freely, drape the lead rope over your arm. Begin by dropping it on the floor directly in front of your horse. Ask your horse to pass your hat. Your horse should pick up the hat straight away and pass it to you, if he does then go nuts with the praise and reward him well. If he doesn't pick it up straight away then bend over and hold the hat just above the floor, your horse should take it from your hand as he did before, repeat until you can rest it on the floor and will pick it up and give it back to you on request. Again, go mad with the praise as soon as he gets this part of the trick. Practise this lesson until he performs it well.

Lesson 5: Next find a reasonably confined area like your horse's stable or small lunging pen. Throw your hat two or three feet away from where you are standing, and ask you horse again to 'pass or fetch your hat'. When your horse obliges and collects the hat reward and praise well, go overboard with the attention to show he has done well. If he doesn't go for the hat, alternate between lesson 4 and 5 until your horse understands what you are asking.

Lesson 6: For this next lesson you want to toss the hat a little farther, perhaps 6 to 8 feet away. Ask your horse to fetch the hat again, whilst pointing to it. If your horse fetches straight away, go berserk with praise and treats. If he doesn't initially try to fetch it, lead your horse over to it and ask him to pick it up again. Repeat this lesson until your horse will successfully retrieve the hat.

Hitting the Bottle!

In this lesson you will ask you horse to hold a soda bottle in the air to pretend he is drinking from it. If you intend to put together a performance, this trick works well in slapstick drunken routine. Just make sure the next time you are out on a hack, your horse doesn't decide to take a detour to the village pub!

Tools Required: - Head Collar, Lead Rope, Whip, Whole Carrots, Large Plastic Unbreakable Soft Drink Bottle, and Clicker.

Lesson 1: Dress your horse in the head collar and lead rope and tie your horse up loosely so he has room to move his head freely. Jam a fat carrot onto the neck of the bottle. Next, standing at your horse's shoulder, gently insert the bottle neck between your horse's lips and ask him to 'Drink Up!' Let him eat the carrot while you continue to ask him to 'Drink Up!' click and tell him what a good boy he is!

Lesson 2: Repeat lesson 1, but on this occasion without the carrot. As soon as the horse tries to grab hold of the bottle neck, click and reward well. Repeat until you horse understands and slowly extend the time he holds the bottle before you acknowledge with the click and treat, then praise to acknowledge your horse has done what you have been aiming for. You horse will appreciate this and strive to get it perfect every time.

Lesson 3: Now that your horse will hold the bottle, you want to combine this with raising the head so your horse looks like he is drinking from the bottle. Ask your horse to take the bottle again but as he does so raise his head by placing your hand under his chin, ask him to 'Drink Up!' again and 'Hold' the pose for a few seconds before clicking and following with the praise and reward.

Lesson 4: Keep rehearsing lesson 3 until your horse will perform it well. You can replace the hand held under the chin with your schooling whip as a reminder to hold his head up. Extend the length of time your horse poses with the bottle. Begin slowly with a few seconds, working toward 10 to 15 seconds, depending on how thirsty you want him to look for his trick performances.

Lesson 5: Soon your horse will perform on the verbal prompt 'Drink Up' and will hold the position until he hears a click or a 'Good Boy' signalling the end of the pose.

Had a Drink Have We?

Are you sure your horse hasn't broken into the cider apple orchard when you weren't looking!

Masters of the trick horse comedy routines occasionally use this easy trick creatively, to make the horse appear intoxicated. This can be practiced and extended in impressive and demanding routines such as pivot on and off the training pedestal and combined with other tricks such as holding the soda bottle for greater effect.

Tools Required: Head-collar, Lead rope, 12ft Soft Yacht Braid Rope, Schooling Whip, Protective Boots or Leg Bandages, Favourite Treats.

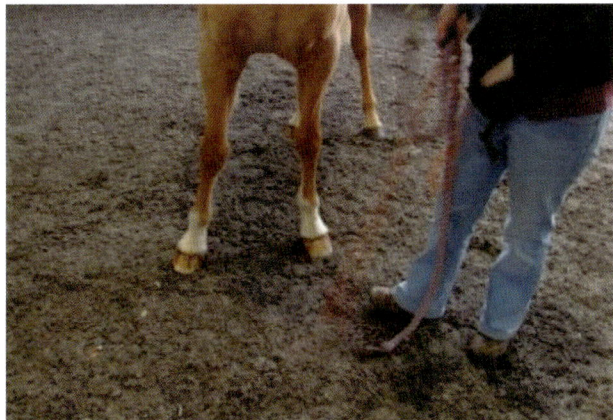 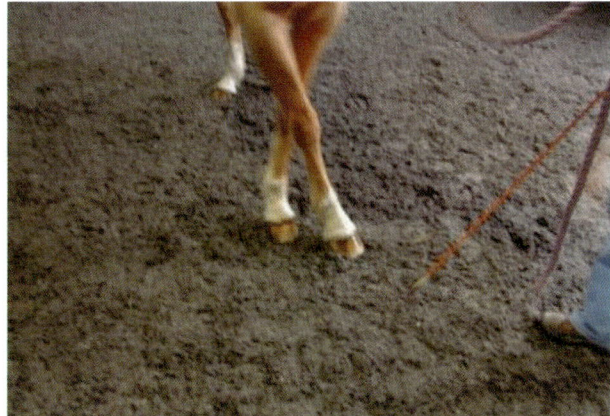

Lesson 1: Dress your horse in the head collar, lead rope and boots for protection. Find a quiet area such as the horse's own stable where he can relax and concentrate. Position him with his right side against a wall to limit unwanted movement. Stand at your horse's left shoulder and loop the snap end of the soft 12 foot training rope around your horse's right pastern holding the slack in your hand. Gently pull on the rope to encourage the right foot to cross in front of the left and give the verbal cue 'Pass'. As soon as your horse crosses his legs reward well and make a big fuss of him.

Lesson 2: Practice lesson 1 until only the lightest pressure on the rope is required to prompt the desired response. At this point you can introduce the whip cue. Apply a tap to the pastern as you say the verbal cue 'pass', immediately before you give a gentle prompting pull on the rope. Again, treat well every time the horse tries for you.

Lesson 3: By now your horse should be associating the tap on the pastern with the word 'pass' and will offer the leg movement. Only use the rope at this stage as a prompt if necessary. Keep repeating this, in short 5 minute sessions, rewarding as you progress until the horse moves the foot on the whip tap and verbal command only.

Lesson 4: The rope can now be removed and practise can continue without it. Slowly increase the amount of time the horse holds the position by asking him to 'stay' and gradually with holding the treat for increasingly longer periods. If he moves before you are ready, say 'no' and position him correctly again before clicking and rewarding.

Lesson 5: Once your horse has mastered this move in one direction, swap sides and ask him to try it with the other leg. You will most likely need to repeat the training again from lesson 1 but your horse should catch on quick. Next, refresh your horse with the 'Hitting the Bottle' trick. (pg 78)

Lesson 6: Now ask your horse to cross over the legs and before clicking, ask him to take the bottle in his mouth whilst raising his head. Request your horse to hold the bottle for a couple of seconds before, clicking, rewarding and praising well. Repeat the lesson, asking your horse to hold the pose for longer and longer periods before clicking and rewarding. The time should be gradually increased.

Lesson 7: Now ask you horse to stand square. Request he takes the bottle and performs the drinking pose. Once in position, hold the schooling whip under the horse's chin to encourage him to keep his head held high. Next, cue him to cross his legs! This may take several attempts, but as soon as you have the slightest try, click, reward, and praise well. If the horse drops the bottle or lowers his head, go back to the beginning and repeat until your horse understands. The moment your horse succeeds, make sure he knows it with lots of treats and love! You now have a fantastic drinking buddy who can hold it with the best of them!

The Flag Wave

A novel combination trick which teaches the horse to pick something up in his mouth, hold a pose requested of him or wave it by cueing the 'Yes' or 'No' trick. Your patriotic horse will be able to support his local riding club by carrying the team flag with pride.

Tools Required: Head Collar, Lead Rope, Stick Flag, Whip, Clicker, Treats

Lesson 1: Refresh your horse with the 'Yes' or 'No' trick depending on which direction you want your horse to eventually wave the flag. Also revisit the 'Hold' trick but, in this instance, you want the horse to hold the stick of the flag.

Lesson 2: Now dress your horse in his head collar and lead and hold the rope in your left hand whilst you position yourself at your horse's left hand shoulder. **Important:** Next slowly introduce your horse to the flag; this is best done in a sheltered area out of the wind such as your stable, to avoid your horse getting startled by fabric flapping in the breeze. Let you horse sniff and get familiar with the flag, as soon as your horse is brave enough to sniff it and touch it with the nose, click, and reward and praise your horse. Repeat until he will confidently approach and play with it.

Lesson 3: Ask your horse to take the flag stick in his mouth and hold it. Reinforce the 'Hold' command by holding your hand under his chin or by holding it in his mouth so your horse doesn't drop the stick, whilst doing so praise him and keep repeating the 'Hold' command. Keep this short to begin with but you can increase the length of time you insist on the hold as your lessons progress. When you are ready for your horse to give the flag back, ask for it by gently taking it from the mouth and politely saying 'Thank you'. When you have it, click, and praise and treat well. Taking the flag before it is dropped will reinforce in your horse's mind that he is to keep hold of it until you ask for it back.

Note: If your horse does drop the flag before you ask for it back, tell him 'No' in a disapproving voice and quickly retrieve it and ask him to 'Hold' it again straight away. Your horse will soon learn if he drops it he gets no reward and a negative response in your tone of voice. By holding on to it until you ask for it back he will get lots of attention, fussing, a click and his due reward.

Lesson 4: Repeat lesson 3 gradually increasing the length of time you ask for the hold before requesting it back. Be sure if the flag is dropped you show your disapproval in a consistent way and repeat the exercise. This will be increasing in very small stages from, a second, two seconds, 5 seconds, 10 seconds etc and then all of a sudden you will notice that the horse catches on and won't let go until asked.

Lesson 5: Repeat above until the hold is perfected, you can then start having fun asking your horse to combine this trick with others, such a shaking the head for 'No' to wave the flag.

Little Pick-Pocket

This is a combination trick that makes use of 'Targeting techniques' and 'Hold the target object' tricks. It teaches a horse to use his mouth. It also teaches a horse to look for and retrieve a specific object to gain a reward. This can be applied to almost any object your can think of! Just watch your wallet! You can even apply this to getting your horse to bring you his feed bucket. Take care though when asking your horse to retrieve an item from your person that he doesn't nip by accident.

Tools Required: - Head Collar, Lead Rope, Handkerchief, Clicker & Treats

Lesson 1:- First ensure your horse understands the 'Hold a target object' trick (page 73). You need to ensure your horse will grab hold of an object held under his nose and not drop it until requested to do so.

Lesson 2:- Introduce the handkerchief to you horse. Hold it under his nose until he sniffs and nuzzles it telling him 'Hanky!' As soon as you horse touches the hanky, reward him and tell him he is a good boy. Repeat this until you can hold the hanky out in front of you and he will nuzzle the hanky when you say 'Where's the Hanky'. He will quickly realise as soon as you say the cue word 'hanky', he is to touch it to get his reward.

Lesson 3:- Now you need to make him look for the hanky. Keep it simple at first, hang it on the stable door or on the fence and move a couple of feet away from it. Say again 'Where's the hanky?' your horse will probably think about this for a few minutes before he moves to nuzzle the hanky on the door. As soon as he does reward him well, and give him lots of praise because his light bulb has now come on in his head. He has got it! Repeat this for the next few days, practise in the stable with your horse loose so you can place it a bit further away and in different places encouraging your horse to find it. Again, reward every time he nuzzles the hanky. Note: Don't conceal the hanky; it must always be in view!

Lesson 4:- Now it's time to combine the above steps with the 'Holding an Object' trick. Hold the hanky in your hand and ask him to nuzzle it again. Reward as soon as he does as asked. Now hang the hanky on the wall next to you and ask him again. Reward as soon as he touches it. Now this time place the hanky in the top of your trousers or tuck it into your belt on your hip. Ask again 'Where's the hanky?' as soon as he nuzzles it on your hip, reward him again. Repeat!

Lesson 5:- Now your horse understands what the 'Hanky' is and he can & will look for it because he knows he will be rewarded when he finds and touches it. Next, you want him to hold the hanky.

To do this, take the hanky holding it under his nose again, but this time, ask him to 'Hold'. If you have taught the 'Hold the Object' trick well, he should take it in his teeth and not drop it until asked.

Lesson 6:- Repeat lesson 5 until your horse completes it successfully. Now you need to combine everything to train your little pick-pocket! Tuck the hanky into your belt or waist-band on your hip, and ask you horse to 'Hold the Hanky'. NOTE: Be careful at this stage as occasionally your horse may get a bit excited and nip you by accident when trying to grab the hanky. Also be aware that your horse may tear what you are wearing if he grabs the material with the hanky so it is wise to wear something old that you don't mind getting torn. Your horse should now know to look for the hanky and take it in his teeth! If he nuzzles it but does not take it then you need to keep working on the 'Hold'. Keep repeating step 6, but keep changing where you keep the hanky, change pockets, belt or waistband, shirt pocket etc to give your little pick pocket plenty of practice looking for it.

Lesson 7:- The same method can be used for many different objects, so if you want the horse to take a wallet or your hat etc, Repeat steps 1 to 4 replacing the hanky with the object of your choice so your horse knows to look for it, Then practise step 5, Holding the object, Then combine the two tricks, as per step 6, to get your sneaky little friend to take the object from you!

Trick Tip:- In order to make the hanky more appealing, wrap up the treats you will be using inside the hanky and leave overnight before training. The hanky will smell delicious to your horse and he will just have to investigate!

Play Ball!

This is a fun game for your horse that helps to improve your horse's coordination and confidence around strange and unusual objects. Your horse may prove to be a budding Premiership football star! Once he has mastered pushing and guiding the ball you can use your imagination with other objects such as rolling a barrel, opening doors etc.

Tools required: - Head Collar, Lead Rope, Treats, and Ball (The bigger the better, a heavy duty inflatable gym ball is ideal)

Lesson 1:- Dress your horse in head collar and lead rope. Lead your horse up to the ball with some reassuring encouragement. Most horses will be a little cautious, apprehensive, or even frightened, about the new strange object, so be patient and allow him time to approach and investigate the ball. After a bit of snorting, and advance and retreat behaviour, your horse will eventually pluck up the courage to sniff the ball. Praise and reward well, if you have a clicker, click once and start repeating the verbal cue 'Play Ball!' Keep practicing until your horse will approach the ball easily and you can roll it around gently in front of your horse and against his legs without panic.

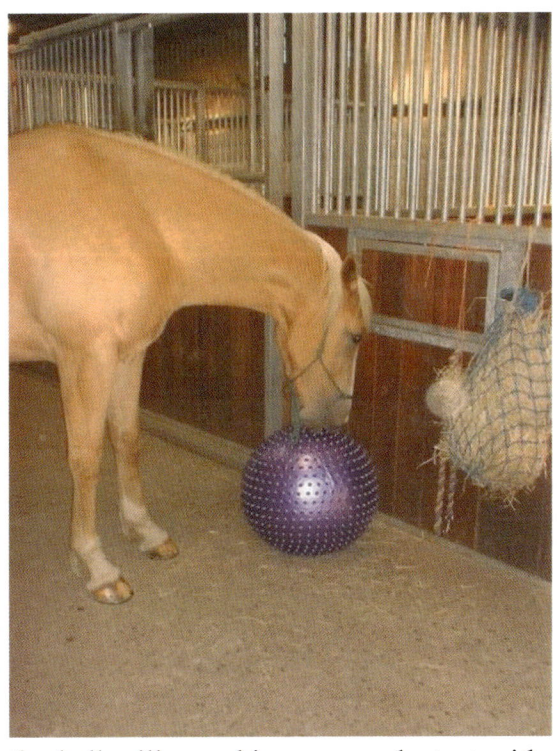

Lesson 2:- Once your horse is confidently approaching the ball, start to encourage him to sniff it, and reward as soon as he touches the ball with his nose. Keep practising until he associates touching the ball with the reward.

Lesson 3:- When your horse clearly recognises touching the ball will earn him a reward, start withholding the treats. Continue asking for him to 'push ball', until he tries to nuzzle the ball a couple of times with the nose. Your horse will be eager to convince you to part with a treat so will try harder. Keep practising and soon on the sight of the ball or your verbal cue you horse will immediately begin to push the ball. Some horses really begin to enjoy this and spend hours playing with the ball in the field or stable. World Cup here we come!

Lesson 4:- Now that your horse has earned his football jersey, this same trick technique can be used on a variety of objects such as rolling a barrel, opening a door etc. Just ensure that for every new object you introduce to your horse, you remember to spend the time familiarising him with the new toy so he is completely at ease and enjoys himself.

Chapter 5: Clever Clogs

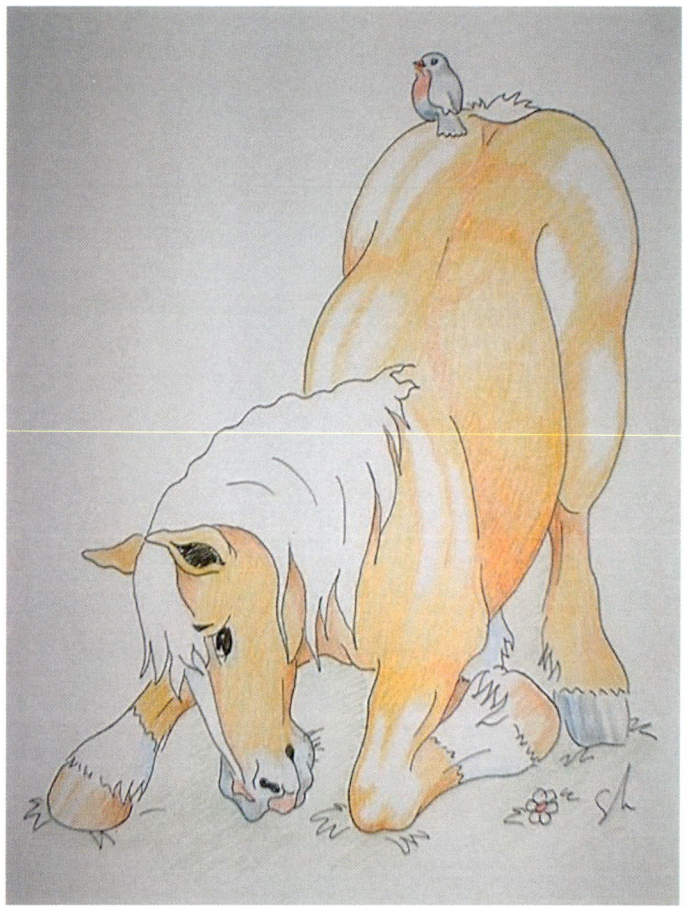

Congratulations! If you have successfully completed chapter 4 then you and your little student should both be feeling very proud of yourselves. The tricks you have mastered should by now have opened your eyes to how easy and rewarding this training can be. I am sure you will have noticed your communication and relationship has improved. Indeed, you should both be getting a deeper respect for one another as partners!

I hope you can see your horse is surprisingly capable of more than you thought possible. It is now time to move on to some of the classic tricks. The type of tricks we associate with circus, display, and dressage divas!

These will test you as much as the horse. They will take more time and patience to master, so you must stick with it and keep your goals in sight. Practise regularly and always finish on a good note. If your horse does what you ask, reward him well and stop the lesson there! We want him to remember the things he has done well. By stopping at that point you are giving positive reinforcement to his actions rather than continuing to nag him to do it again and again which will bore and lead to resentment from your horse!

The following tricks are the stuff of the dream horse. Everyone would love to teach these but very few know how. Follow each trick in order and move at your horse's own pace, never rush or try and cut corners. Be patient and your time and effort will be well rewarded. This is where you can shine as a trainer and your horse can show what a clever clogs he is!

Good Luck!

The Bow 'Obeisance'

Here is one to impress the crowds! A popular trick for any performing horse and a classic in the Circus ring! Make sure your horse is physically mature and fit enough with good muscle coverage before you start. It is also a very good idea, when first learning this, to attempt it after riding or lunging when the horse has been warmed up to help prevent strain to the joints and muscles.

Tools Required: - Head Collar, Normal Lead Rope (Approx 6 Foot), Soft Long Lead Rope (Approx 12 Foot), Surcingle, Whip & Whole Carrots.

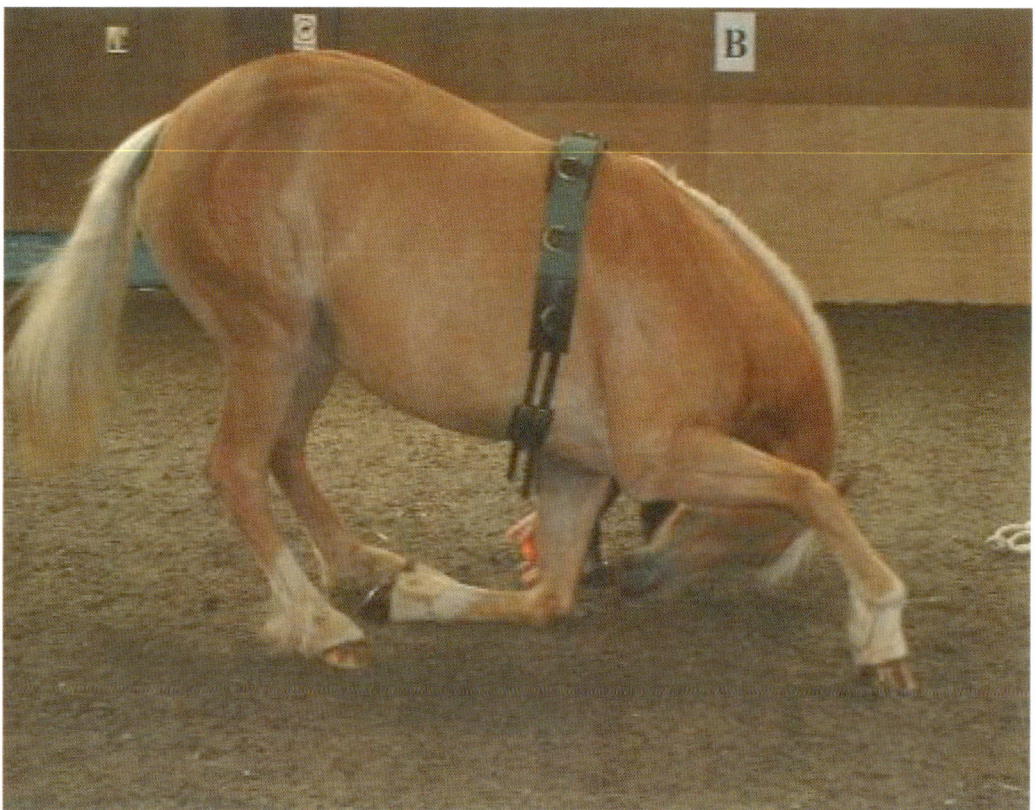

Lesson 1:- In a quiet, roomy area, with a soft floor covering such as a loose box or indoor school, dress your horse in his head collar and lead rope and a securely fitted training surcingle. Take the longer lead rope and loop one end around your friend's near fore pastern, take the other end of the rope and feed it through the highest Dee ring on the surcingle.

Lesson 2:- Standing at your horse's near side shoulder some distance away from any walls, hold your horse steady by holding the normal lead rein in your left hand. Use the right hand, too gently pull on the long rope and ask him to raise his front foot. Take your time with this. It is important that your horse remains calm, comfortable and relaxed. Reward with plenty of praise when he obliges. Keep practising until he holds this pose without objection.

Lesson 3:- Now, with the front foot still raised, begin to entice the horse's head downwards and backwards by holding a carrot between the front legs whilst saying 'Bow'. As your horse tries to reach for the carrot draw it back underneath his body so he horse will follow with his head and has to swing his body weight back and will be tempted to kneel on the raised leg in order to reach the elusive carrot!

As the horse will be unsteady, he may not get to the ground in the first few attempts. Still reward every effort so he knows he is doing well, and will be willing to try that bit harder for you on the next go!

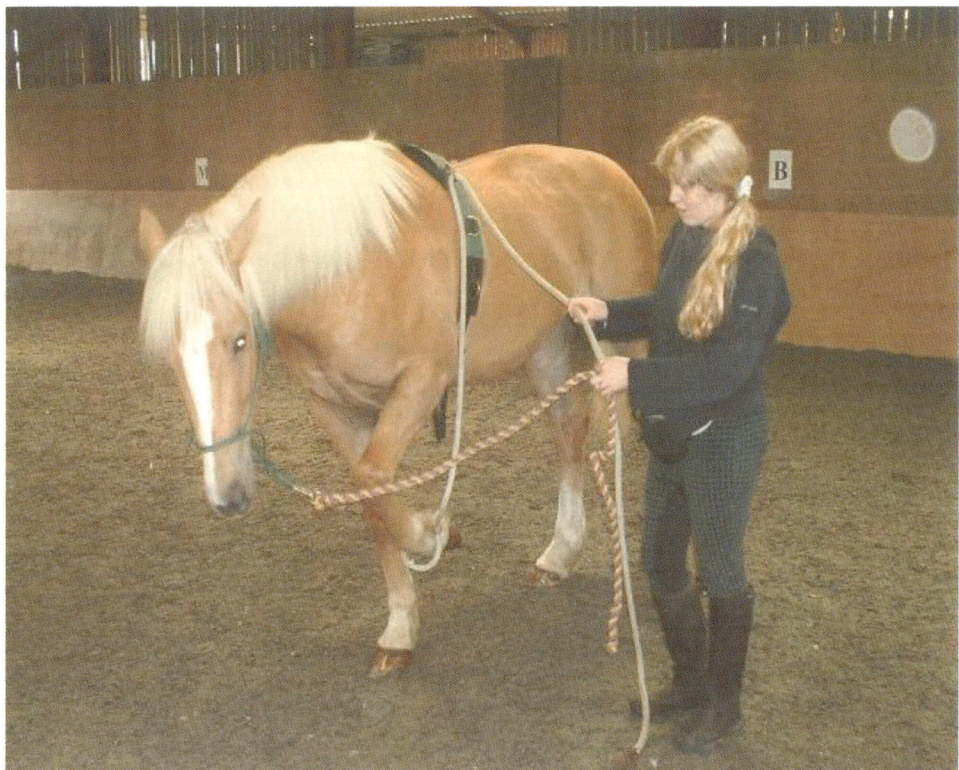

He will soon learn to steady himself to make the job that wee bit easier! Take care that if your horse does stumble or lose his balance that you're ready to calmly but quickly move out of the way, whilst offering a calming and comforting word to your friend.

Lesson 4:- Keep the training session short, approx 5 to 10 minutes a day should be sufficient, especially as your horse will not be used to this movement and the muscles will tire easily. Repeat stages 1 to 3 until he starts to offer the leg lift and bow action just by following the carrot without you having to encourage by pulling on the leg rope.

Lesson 5:- Continue the next few sessions with the horse still dressed in the equipment. Next, we need to introduce the whip cue. Whilst asking the horse to 'Bow', take the whip and lightly tap him on the knee before applying the rest of the aids you have been using up until now. Practise this for the next few sessions so the horse begins to associate the tap on the knee, and vocal command 'Bow', as the prompt to perform this trick

Trick Tip* You may possibly notice at this stage that as soon as the horse goes down, he wants to stand straight back up again. This happens for a variety of reasons. He may be unbalanced and slightly uncomfortable, nervous to be in such a vulnerable position or perhaps there are distractions happening nearby. You can encourage the horse to remain on the knee a little longer by vocally insisting he 'Stay' once down, and only feeding the treat whilst in the correct position. Very light pressure can be placed on the short lead rope to encourage the head to remain down, but do not resist too much on the rope, any fight may make the horse reluctant to try again if he feels trapped.

Lesson 6:- Continue your short sessions until the horse if offering the bow to you on the whip tap and 'Bow' commands. Then, once the horse is happy, dispense with the leg rope completely, and practise on the 'tap and bow' whilst the horse is wearing his head collar, lead, and surcingle. This is to simulate the original training session as much as possible. You are trying to build on the horse's confidence by taking each stage very slowly. Once happy, remove the surcingle and practise just using the head collar, lead, whip and carrot.

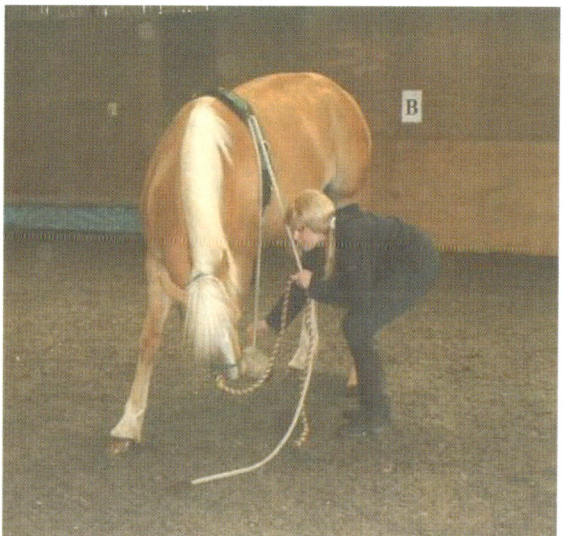
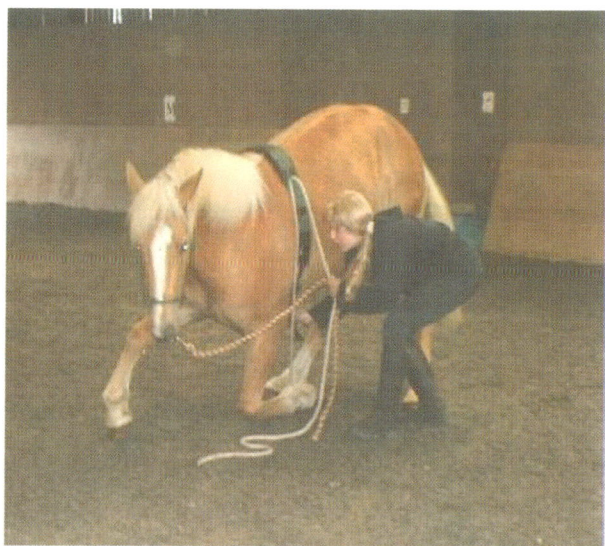

Lesson 7:- To truly polish this trick off, begin by placing a hand just above the point of the withers with gentle downward pressure as you give the verbal cue 'Bow'. Follow this up by the whip cue. Very soon, your position and the gentle pressure of the hand on the withers will prompt the bow. Remember to cease pressure as soon as your horse responds correctly, but leave the hand in place until you wish the horse to rise.

Lesson 8:- On perfecting the above you should give yourself a big pat on the back and your horse a very big hug and praise. This is a big milestone in his trick training! You should also appreciate how much your horse must trust you to willingly submit & relax on request. This is a big compliment to you as a trainer. Once confident, progress this further by removing the lead and collar and practising this at liberty, or try it dressed in his bridle and saddle. This can take several more weeks, but is well worth the effort as it is will look extremely polished and professional!

The Bow under Saddle

Tools Required: - Bridle, Saddle, Schooling Whip, Treats, Protective Boots or Bandages,

Lesson 1:- First ensure the horse knows the bow well in ground training and that the balance is well established. Dress your horse ready for riding, and whilst he is learning ensure he is wearing protective boots or bandage to protect the legs just in case he should lose his balance. Find a willing assistant who has been shown how to ask your horse to 'Bow'. They can then stand on the near side and encourage the horse down for you.

Mount the horse, lean slightly back in the saddle, and ask your assistant to cue the trick as if you were not on board. Any attempt should be rewarded. Remember, the horse has not only got to find his balance, but must also accommodate his passenger. Repeat only once or twice on the early lessons so not to damage the horse's back and joints. Whilst sitting in the saddle the part you play in the movement is as important as your horse's!

Allow your horse an extremely loose rein, (Extra long reins are helpful!) Sit as straight, centred and as calm as possible. As he goes down on one knee concentrate on keeping your back vertical to the ground. Expect your horse to be a bit wobbly the first few times and assist him by remaining relaxed, balanced and full of encouragement and praise for every effort.

Lesson 2:- Repeat Step 1 until the horse can manage it easily and hold for a short time, rewarding on each occasion. Once again, only attempt once or twice per session, to avoid injuries.

Lesson 3:- Now that your horse is performing the movement well, take the schooling whip from your assistant and attempt the same cues from the saddle by leaning gently forward and tapping the left knee with the whip. Your assistant may encourage with a bit of body language and a carrot as before if you have trouble as long as you remain in control of the whip. With regular practise it will soon become easy and a fine performance!

Above:-Lose the ropes, gadgets, elaborate tack and training crutches and what happens next is the truth of your training success and partnership!

Kneeling or 'Arabian Prayers'

Every good horse should learn to pray! This is a variation of the 'Obeisance', and is good preparation for teaching the horse to lie down.

Tools Required: - Head collar, Lead Rope, Soft long lead rope, Schooling whip, Protective boots or bandages, Treats.

Lesson 1:- Dress your horse in head collar and lead rope and stand at his near shoulder. Ask your horse to bow as per the previous lesson and reward.

Lesson 2:- Your timing now is crucial. Ask for the bow again but the second the horse's knee is on the ground, reach across and tap his right knee with the schooling whip whilst commanding the horse to 'Kneel' or 'Pray'. The horse should in theory transfer the meaning of the tap on the knee from one leg to the other and draw the right leg back to perform the kneel. If the horse does as asked, or at least tries for you, let him get back to his feet and reward well with lots of praise.

Lesson 3:- Once kneeling in the correct position, you can decide on how you want your horse to hold his head. Use a treat to draw the head into position, usually down at the chest, whilst emphasising the verbal cue 'Pray'. You can also use this to increase the length of time your horse holds the pose until you are ready for him to get back on his feet.

Lesson 4:- An alternative to the 'Arabian Prayers' is the 'Camel Stretch'. Once your horse is on his knees he can be encouraged to extend his head and neck low out in front resting his chin on the floor by following a juicy carrot. With practise the horse will relax and rest his elbows on his heels dropping the front end closer to the ground.

This is an interesting variation mainly because very few people seem to practise this pose. It is probably not as natural to the horse as the majority of tasks in this book so it speaks volumes about the trusting partnership you have with your horse.

Bottoms Up!

Lie Down

*Above: **The ultimate chilled horse!** -This is the hard life of a trick horse.*

This is the true test of ultimate horsemanship. By this stage your horse must have complete trust and confidence in you to put himself in such a vulnerable position on request.

Using your imagination you can have a lot of fun with this trick or it can be used for practical reasons. Occasionally horses are trained to lie down to assist riders with disabilities to mount with ease. Or a horse that is injured or tangled in fencing can be asked to relax and lie down to reserve energy and minimise injury and distress whilst they are being rescued.

This is my preferred method that works by encouraging the horse's natural desire to roll, and moulding the behaviour to be re-enacted on cue. Be warned though, this method is time consuming and will test your patience so be prepared to put in the time.

Achieving the lie down in this manner, by patience and communication you demonstrate ultimate horsemanship, partnership and trust. Other methods, which include force and hobbling, only prove that you can conquer, bully, and dominate.

Tools required:- Patience of a Saint, Head-collar, and long lead rein, schooling whip, clicker, treats.

Lesson 1:- Turn the horse loose in an enclosure with a soft floor surface where the horse might be encouraged to roll. Stand back and observe your horse's behaviour closely. You want to promote the idea that it might be a good time to roll. Before a horse thinks of lying down he will sniff the floor and paw at the ground. Any offering of this behaviour should be

encouraged with verbal praise or if the horse recognises the clicker, then a click when appropriate. The horse realising you like him putting his nose to the ground will offer the behaviour more and more. In natural circumstances, a horse walking around with his nose to the floor will begin to question why. Your horse's natural instinct tells him to lie down.

Continue encouraging your horse to lower his head and hopefully lie down on his own by telling him to 'lie down'. This is a waiting game. Stay there until the horse rolls. As soon as your horse is down, carefully approach, encouraging you horse to stay down by offering a treat and loads of praise whilst he is on the floor and then clicking the clicker box. As soon as the horse get to his feet praise him again and call it a day so you horse can think about what he just did that pleased you.

Lesson 2:- Repeat lesson one several times off the lead. Stand back and continually ask your horse to 'lie down'. Every time your horse drops the nose to the ground, praise him as he is moving in the right direction. Treat it as a game of hot and cold, the warmer he gets to the ultimate goal, the more praise you lavish on him. You will notice that after a couple of sessions like this the horse will begin to lie down a lot more quickly.

Lesson 3:- Once you can get the horse to lie down within minutes, start the next session on a long lunge line. Stand in the centre and leave the line relatively loose so your horse has freedom to move around. Raise your end of the rope quite high to keep any slack away from your horse's front feet because if you don't the horse might catch it with a foreleg when he starts to paw at the ground. Repeat your verbal cue to 'lie down' again praising any lowering of nose, or pawing of the ground, until the horse goes down. Again, reward him as soon as he is on the floor with his treat and buckets of praise! End the lesson on this as a reward for the horse getting the right answer.

Lesson 4:- Repeat lesson three until the horse goes down relatively quickly, then ask for the behaviour two or three times in one session.

Lesson 5:- Practice lesson 4 placing more and more emphasis on the cues you have been using, the verbal cue 'lie down!', the raising of the rope, and the tapping of the schooling whip on the ground.

Lesson 6:- Now that your horse is going down well, you want to keep him down until you decide it's time for him to get up. This can be encouraged by only rewarding the horse when he is on the floor and with-holding the treat for longer and longer periods while you verbally ask your horse to stay.

Above: Only a relaxed and trusting horse will lie down for you. The relaxed horse is a joy to work with, ready and willing to listen! Great for that special photo!

1) Horse drops his nose, sniffs and paws the ground when he is considering going down. Look for quarters dropping, bringing the hind legs underneath the belly with a rounded outline whilst nose still on the floor.

2) Once the decision has been made to lie down the hind legs come further under the body, quarters begin to sink and the horse prepares to drop the front end onto the knees.

3) Once on the knees the quarters soon follow.

4) The ultimate goal, down and relaxed!

Once you have mastered the Lie Down, you can test yourself and your horse's trust in you though numerous variations and tricks. For instance:-

- Mounting your horse whilst he is down, then asking him to rise to his feet. This is an easy manoeuvre for the horse and is useful for the rider who has trouble mounting in the normal way.
- Standing on the horse, tests his trust and resolve to stay until he is asked to move. Note: Care must be taken to place your weight across the strong muscle groups of the back or rump so it is comfortable for your horse. Do not stand directly on bony areas such as the hip or spine.
- Sitting on your horse for the perfect partnership photo.
- Playing Dead! This is done by gentle guiding your horse over with the lead rope so he lays flat………………..Use your imagination and have fun!

Trick Tip: If your horse is not offering any interest in rolling, and the weather is warm enough, hose your horse down first, as we all know after bathing our horses the first thing they love to do is to roll!

1.

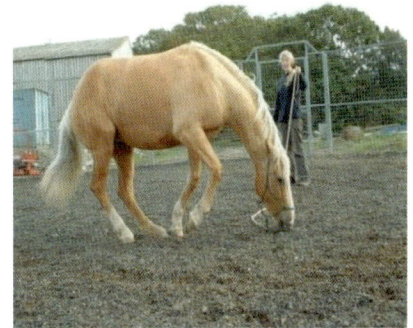

2.

3.

4.

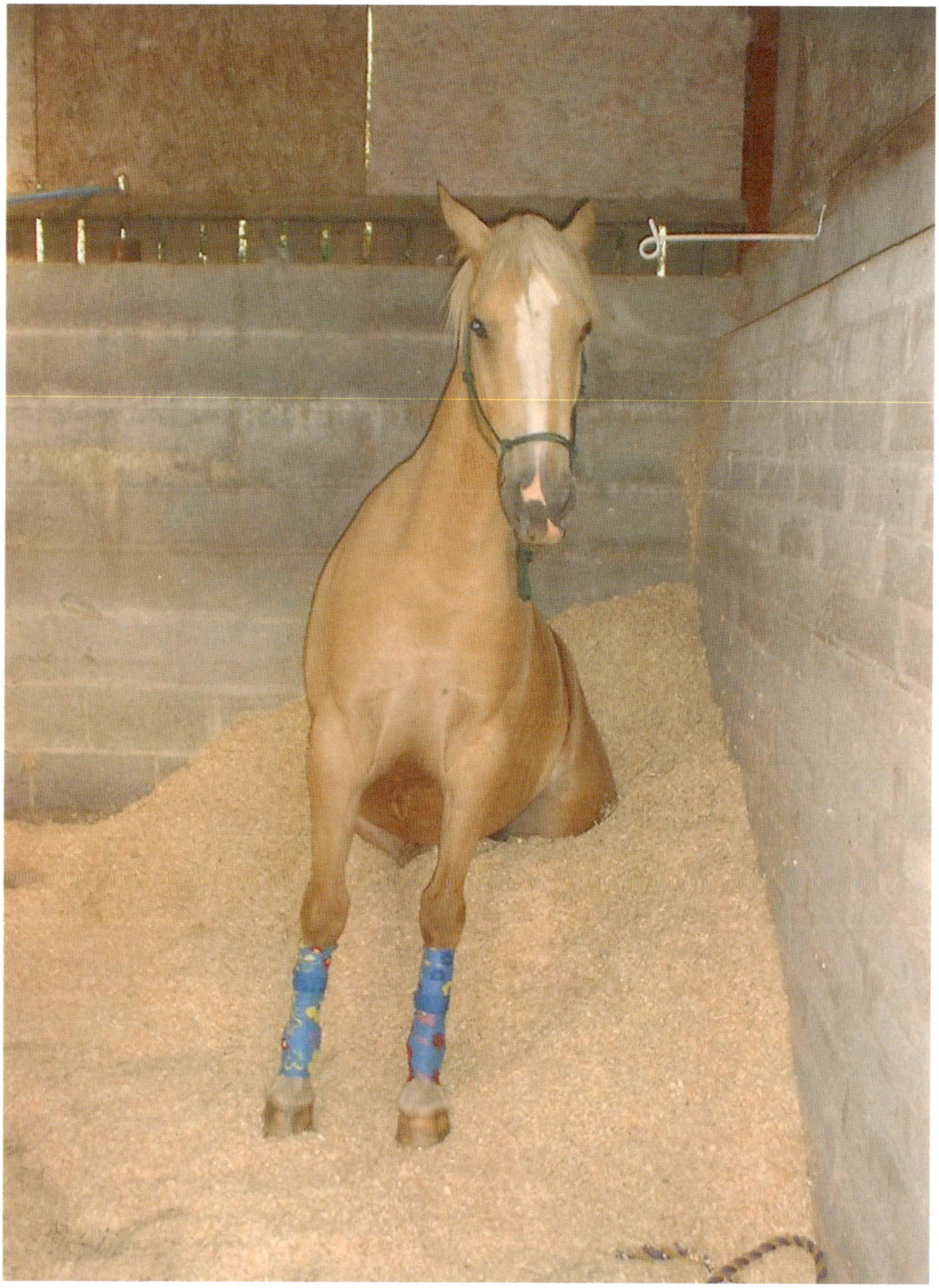

100

Take a Seat

101

A certain crowd pleaser and the perfect training exercise to work on your horse's trust and relaxation. You can literally see your horse relaxing as you work through the lessons. Horses are not particularly flexible creatures and cannot sit down gradually. They must be sure they are safe and that they won't hurt themselves. This is because once a horse starts to sit from a standing position they are more or less committed, as they have to drop their quarters to the floor into that blind area behind the tail.

This is not only a novel trick; it also establishes respect between horse and handler by asking the horse to yield to pressure and respecting your space. This task promotes ultimate trust and relaxation to your horse by encouraging him to accept the request and situation and soften the back and quarters to sink into the correct position. This is ideal when asking your horse to sit on an object like a special beanbag, reinforced prop chair or hay bales.

Although not a natural movement for the horse, it is the quickest way to correct a bolshie, stressed or disrespectful horse

Tools required: - Head collar & Lead Rope or Bridle, Whip, Treats, Bandages or protective boots for your horse, Tail Bandage, Treats.

Lesson 1:- Prepare a corner of your stable or barn with a seat. This should be in the form of a compacted pile of wood shavings or perhaps several bales of hay wrapped in canvas sheeting or tarpaulin. Please ensure whatever you use it is not hard or dangerous to your horse. You need to ensure it is comfortable and that it can take your horse's weight. The photos below show how I prepare a corner of my stable for this training.

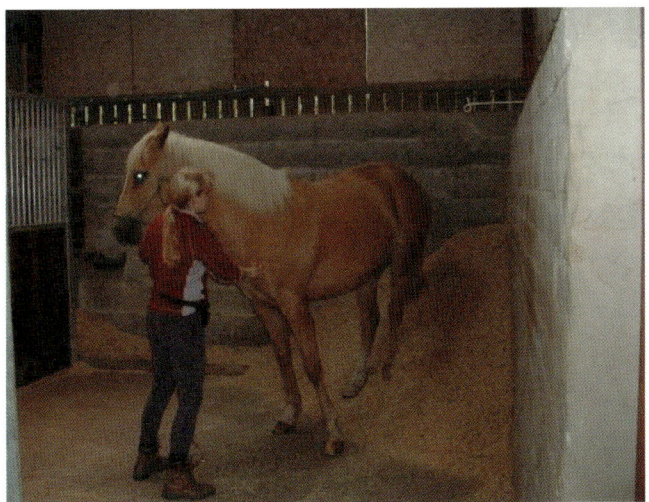
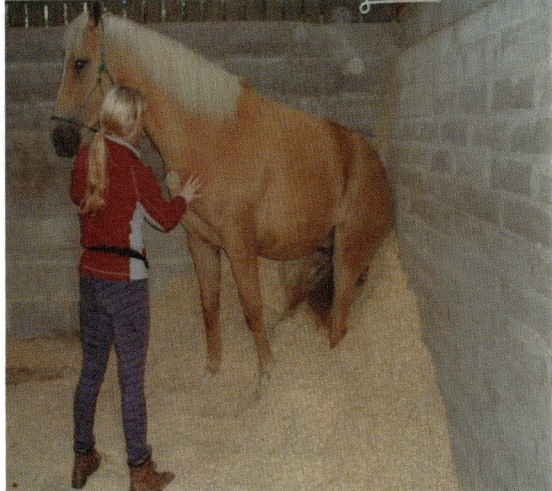

Lesson 2:- Dress your horse in head collar and lead rope. It is also a good idea to train with a tail bandage to protect your horse's locks, as they can get into quite a mess. Start to back your horse up to the shaving pile until his back legs are touching it. As you continue to try and push him backwards your horse will undoubtedly attempt to swing his body in different directions, but you must keep him straight and correct him should this happen, reward him only when he straightens up again with his hind legs touching the shavings.

Lesson 3:- Repeat step 2, keep pushing him backwards into the shaving until you see the quarters rest against the wall. This will take some time so be patient. Your horse needs to relax in this position so, as soon as there is contact with the wall, reward and praise highly, and then walk your horse forward. Be aware that until your horse relaxes there is the possibility of panic flight instinct, as you are pushing him into a corner. So be prepared in case your horse should panic and dash forward, or rear upwards. Do not scold. Remember, to the horse, you are trapping him in a corner. It will take time and praise for him to relax and follow your directions. This may take many practice sessions.

Lesson 4:- Continue with step 3 until your horse will happily reverse into the corner and bare his weight by leaning his quarters against the wall. Now your horse is beginning to show acceptance you can take it a stage further. Position your horse with quarters against the wall and continue to ask him to step backwards. Your horse will come up against resistance from the shavings and the wall; again, he may panic, but persevere with your gentle reassurance and with constant gentle backwards pressure. Any attempt to move backward should be rewarded. This part takes persistence; your horse will want to move forward or upward. Keep the gentle pressure on until you see the back start to round and your horse start to sink his quarters so it would appear that he is sitting on the hocks. As soon as this happens praise him immediately with loads of love and treats so he identifies that by reversing as asked and relaxing in this way he has done a good thing!

Lesson 5:- When your horse is happily sinking onto the hocks in the shavings, continue applying gentle backwards pressure. This may take a few minutes. Watch your horse's quarters, as he relaxes you will start to see them sink down into the shavings. Progress will be very gradual, so ensure you continue with the praise and rewarding with treats. Any minute now he will decide it will be easier to sit down, than continue to stand in this awkward position. As soon as your horse sits, praise well, reward, and try and hold the position for a minute whilst feeding more and more treats for being so good!

Lesson 6:- Don't let your horse remain down for too long on the first few occasions, in case the new strange position affects the circulation in the legs. You will find your horse may have trouble getting back to his feet on the first few occasions, if this is the case let him take his time, stand clear in case he stumbles getting back to his feet and reward by saying thank you and turning out so he can ponder the lesson.

Lesson 7:- As you horse gets better, start to introduce the cue of raising the horse's chin and tapping the quarters whilst giving the verbal command to 'Sit'. In the meantime you can slowly reduce the size of the shavings pile so your horse gets closer to the ground, always remember to provide a cushioned service before asking your horse to sit from the stand so it is comfortable and your friend does not damage his legs or tail bone! Remember he trusts your directions and wants to believe that you will not ask for anything that will cause him harm. It only takes one bad experience to undo all your hard work and to lose that precious trust.

Training Tip: - Once your horse has sat for the first time, only reward him when he is sitting so your horse identifies the action with the reward and therefore should remain sitting until asked to rise.

Sit Up Please!

Horses naturally adopt the sit position we are looking for, as they rise to their feet after lying down. The head is raised and the front legs are braced out in front of them whilst lifting the front of their torso off the floor.

The difference between this cue and the 'Sit from Standing' trick is the horse will be sitting on the ground, rather than a cushioned object.

Tools Required:- Head Collar, Long 12ft lead rope, schooling whip, clicker, treats, Steel toe capped boots for your own protection.

Lesson 1:- First ensure that your horse fully understands and executes the request to lie down, and remains lying down until you invite him to rise to his feet again. The more training he has on this the easier it will be to control the speed that your horse gets back on his feet and, hence, easier for him to pause when asked.

Lesson 2:- Once you are happy he has mastered the cue to lie down and remain there until told to move, you can progress to the next lesson. Dress your horse in head collar and the long lead rope and take him to a quiet area where you won't be disturbed. Make sure the training area has a soft floor away from walls, fences, or anything else that may get in the way or cause injury.

Now ask your partner to lie down again. When you're ready, stand at your horse's shoulder, make sure you have a treat and clicker ready in your spare hand and the lead rein in the other. Ask your horse to start getting up slowly while you control the speed with a steady gentle pressure on the lead. At this point, I just wish to warn you that the horse will throw out his front legs to brace for the rise, so watch your feet. It is a good idea to wear steel toe capped boots to protect your feet.

As your horse gets up, you will note the front legs are thrown out in front and he will lift his front end by bracing the front legs. As your horse approaches the sitting position, click and ask him to 'sit & stay' like you would a puppy. Continue to apply slight downward pressure on the lead rein to encourage him to pause for a moment. If he pauses at all, reward immediately whilst holding the position, so your horse will associate the pause and position with his treat. However, most horses will continue to rise until they learn to predict and expect the 'Stay' command from practice. As soon as you have any success, reward, and put your horse away.

Lesson 3: Repeat the lesson until your horse comfortably sits when asked and will remain there until you ask him to rise to his feet.

Lesson 4:- Now your little star pupil has completed his coursework, you can now ask him to try for extra credit! The sitting pose can be made more exciting by your interaction. Repeat the earlier lessons asking your horse to remain in position until you can work around him without him moving, and reward when he happily complies.

Lesson 5:- Next you can either mount from the sitting position, or sit down gently on his haunches whilst calmly reassuring your friend. Sit for a count of three and quietly get off, cue for him to get to his feet, click, praise, and reward your four legged-friend well.

1. Ask your horse to lie down in the upright position and stay. Click and reward.

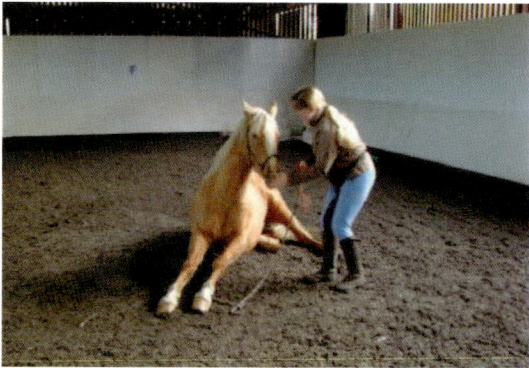

2. Steady your horse with a treat under the nose and slowly ask for the sit up.

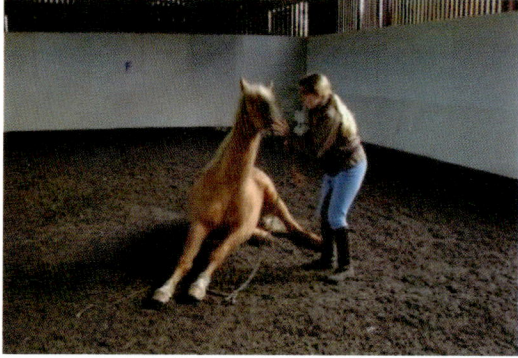

3. Keep a steady pressure on the lead to control the speed your horse rises to his feet.

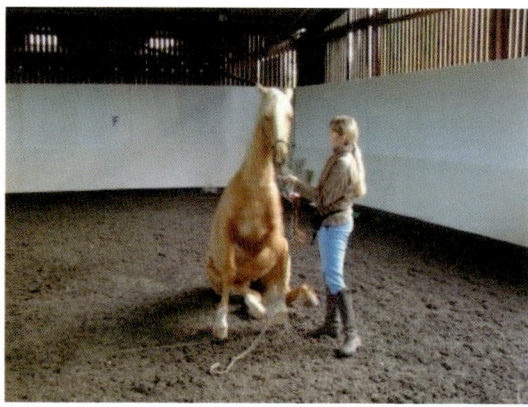

5. Once your horse reaches position click, reward & praise well.

Lesson 6: Practise lesson 5 until you can remain on your horse for some time before getting off and asking him to rise. When your horse is truly comfortable and you are feeling confident and brave enough, you may even wish to try mounting him from this position and asking him to rise beneath you. If your horse appears to struggle with this, it is likely he is not strong or fit enough, and it is best to dismount before asking him to rise.

Lesson 7: For the finale, how about standing on you horse. Firstly, ensure you are wearing soft non-slip shoes that won't dig in or bruise your horse. If they are in anyway uncomfortable, your horse will soon let you know and, understandably, won't want to cooperate. Also please ensure your horse is big enough and old enough to handle your weight, if you can ride him, this should not be an issue. Standing on a youngster can seriously hurt him due to soft and growing bones. Also, it is unwise to use polishing grooming products on these areas that would make the coat slippery.

Ask your horse to sit up again and gently step up onto his haunches with one foot either side of the hip area. Don't stand on the bony area, but rather on the well muscled areas. (NOTE: This area is also one of the last to move should your horse get up unexpectedly so you can easily hop off, if necessary). Hold this for a few seconds and quietly step off. Ask him to stand up and click, praise and reward him again well.

Lesson 8:-Repeat lesson 7 until you can remain standing on the haunches for short periods for the applause or photo shoot!

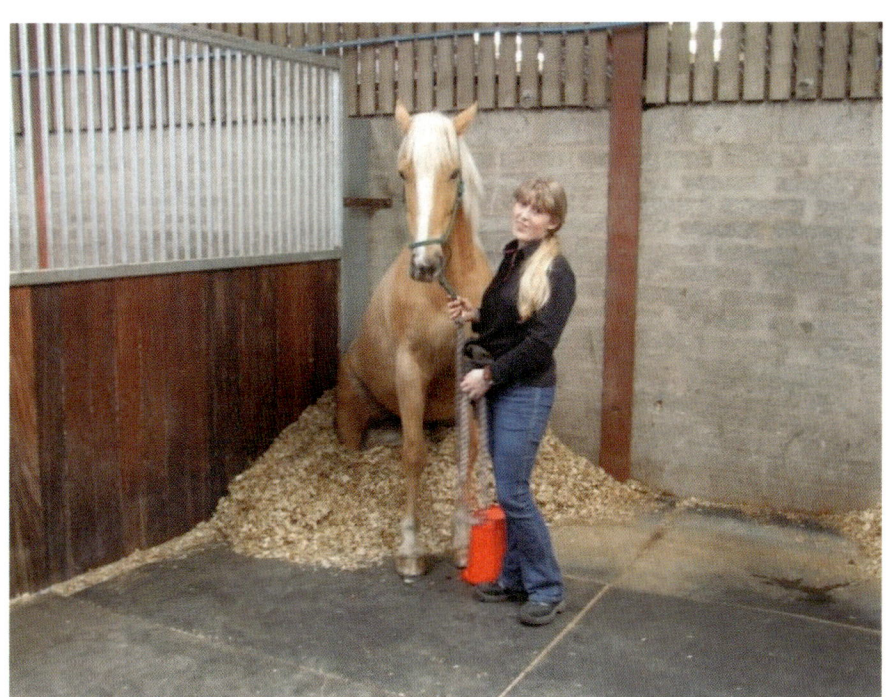

Curtsy or Circus Bow

The Curtsy, also known as the Circus Bow, is a movement that gained its popularity under the Big Top. The object of this trick is for the horse to place his head between outstretched front legs whilst swinging his weight backwards onto the quarters. This is an excellent movement to strengthen, stretch and supple the neck, leg, and back muscles. Take care not to practice too often in the early stages to avoid strains and injury. It will take time for the muscles to build up and for the horse to learn to plant each foot in the right place and to execute correctly, with the face near the floor.

Tools required: - Head Collar & Lead rope, schooling whip, Treats (Whole Carrots to prevent your fingers getting nibbled by accident)

Lesson 1:- First stand your horse up square and insist they stand nice and still. You must first teach your horse to spread his front legs enough so he can place his head between them. To do this, stand at your horse's shoulder and hook your ankle around the inside of your horse's pastern and gently nudge the hoof outwards with gentle pressure, don't force it or the horse will resist it. Click and reward any attempt to move the hoof out to the side.

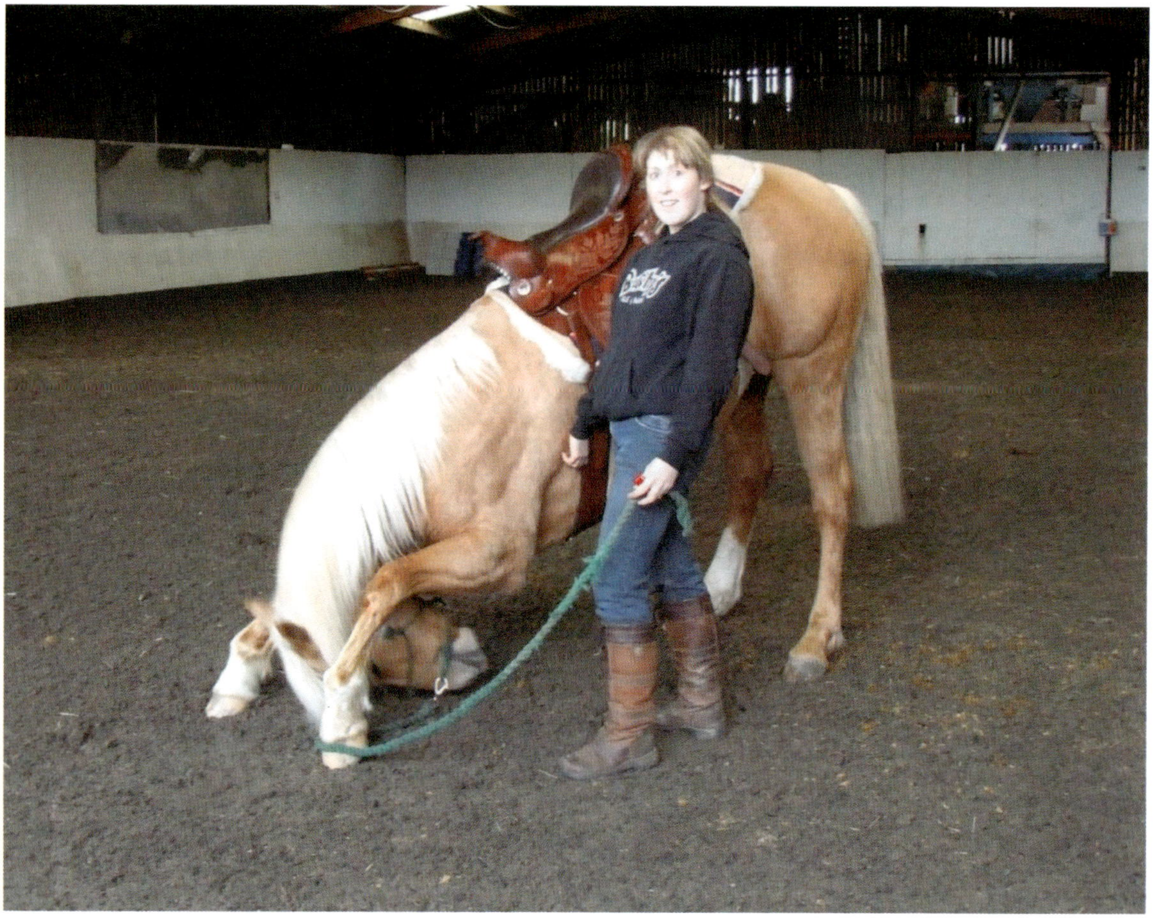

Lesson 2:- Once the horse can stand still with legs far enough apart, you must teach your horse to lower his head to the floor. This is done by gentle downward pressure on the lead rope. Any effort by the horse to drop his head should be rewarded by an immediate release of pressure and a reward. Keep practising till the nose is nearly on the floor and the horse will keep the head there until told to move. Whilst doing this ensure your horse remains Standing Square. This lesson make take several attempts, as the horse will undoubtedly try to offer the bow by starting to raise one leg, if this happens say 'NO' and stand him up square again before re-attempting.

Lesson 3:- Next stand at your horse's near shoulder with lead rope in your left hand and a treat and the schooling whip in your right. Begin by asking for the square stance and requesting the horse to drop the nose to the floor using slight downward pressure from the left hand on the lead rope. Next, tap the horse gently on the chest with the whip and ask for 'Curtsy'. Hold the treat between, and just behind, the fore legs to encourage your horse's nose backwards. Reward any effort to follow but insist the legs stay square. Should the horse attempt to bow, discourage by standing the horse back up and starting again.

Lesson 4:- Keep practising Lesson 3 until the horse keeps his feet in place and you can draw the treat further back under the body and encourage your horse to follow it back with his nose and to swing his weight back onto the quarters. Try to limit to approximately 3 attempts per session whilst in early training to avoid excessive strain and injury. The horse must practise, little and often, to build up the strength to hold the pose for longer periods.

Show your horse how to spread the front legs prior to dropping the head by guiding one foot over with your boot and rewarding well! This will give the horse the room to place his head between his legs! Every horse adds their own twist to a trick; Fern has difficulty straightening her legs so gives what is almost a Michael Jackson signature dance move on her toes!

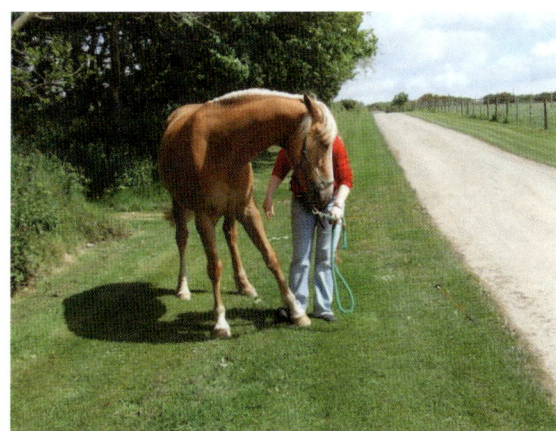
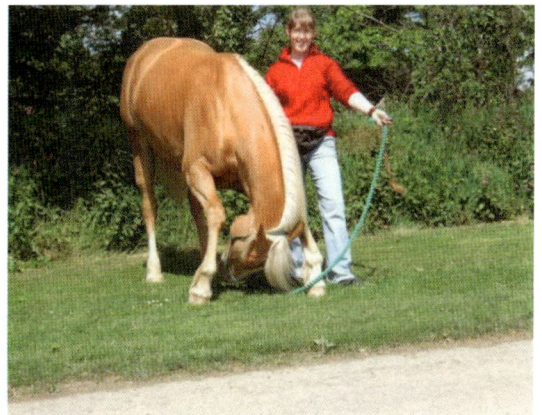

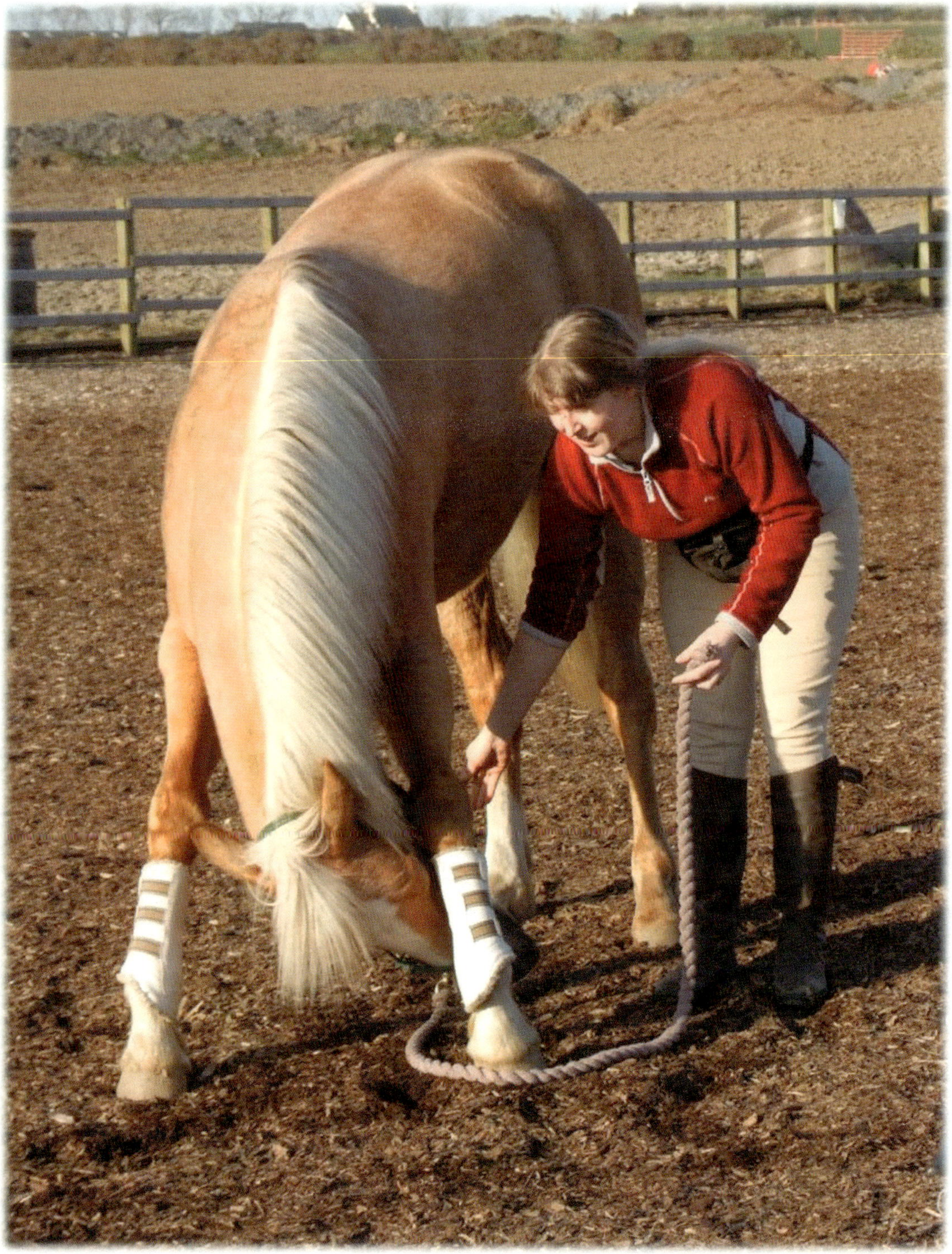

110

Queen's Curtsy

This trick I name the Queens Curtsy. It's a variation of the Bow and the Drunken Stagger Trick. Due to its unusualness, complexity, and the strength required, it is definitely an impressive trick.

Be careful when first starting the Bow section that you teach this slowly, so the horse has time to accustom himself to the odd position and indeed, for his muscles and joints to get used to this new exercise, as you do not want any strains or injuries. For this reason it is probably best to practise this after your horse has been warmed up from exercise.

Tools Required: Head Collar, Lead Rope, Schooling Whips, Treats, Splint Boots, and Clicker.

Lesson 1: Begin by dressing your horse in head collar and lead rope and protective boots. Next, refresh yourselves with the Curtsy Bow and the Drunken Stagger Trick. Ensure both tricks are performed easily and well before moving on to lesson 2.

Lesson 2: Next, ask you horse to adopt the Drunken Stagger position. In this trick, we want the horse to cross the front legs and hold the position. Some horses can find this difficult so try and be patient.

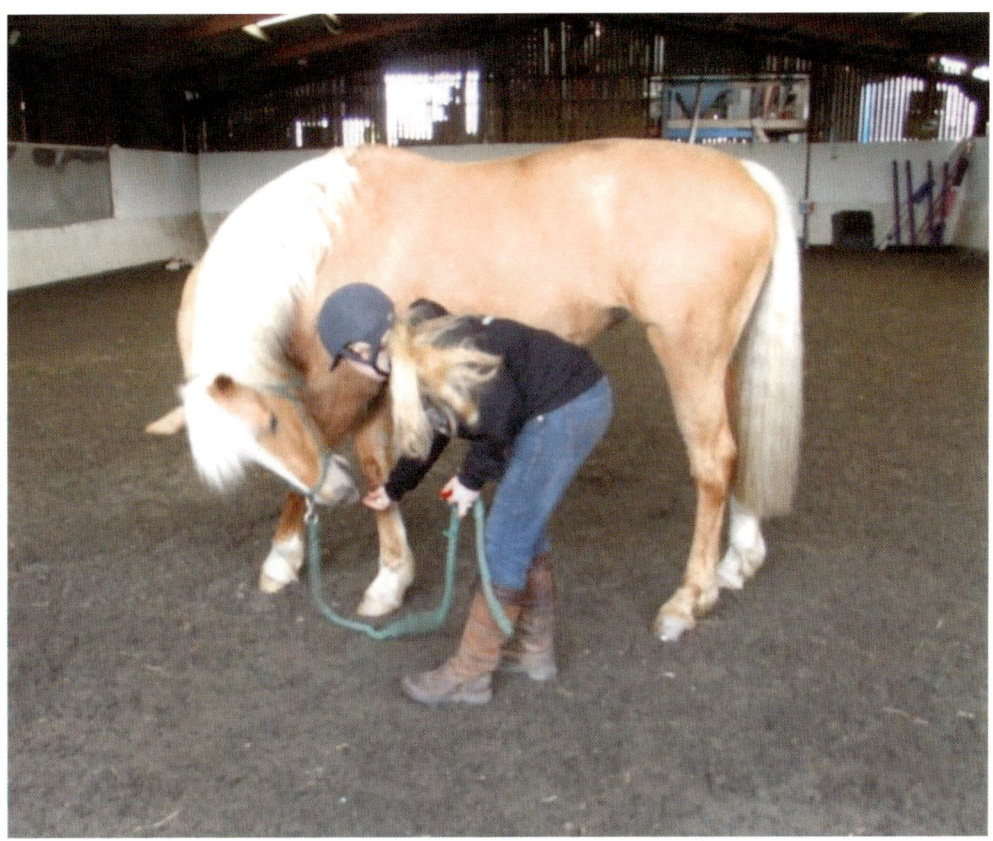

With your left hand on the lead clip, hold the schooling whip in your right hand, and ask for the cross over. As soon as your horse puts the forward leg on the floor, ask him to 'stay', whilst applying gentle steady pressure on the lead clip and horse shoulder. Click and praise well if your horse pauses. He is unlikely to hold this long in the first few attempts, but keep at it and your horse will soon start to predict the stay command and be ready to stop when you ask for it. As soon as this happens, click, treat, and praise well.

Lesson 3: Practise lesson 2 until you horse will stand and hold the position when asked. You will find when your horse fully understands and has mastered the necessary coordination and balance that he will find it easy and actually volunteer the behaviour for a reward. At this stage, ask your horse to hold the cross legged position again, and this time request that he drops his nose to the floor by gentle downward pressure. As soon as your horse complies, praise, click and reward. Repeat as necessary until you can get your horse to hold this entire position for 10 seconds. This may happen quickly or take several sessions, but praise and reward for every successful lesson.

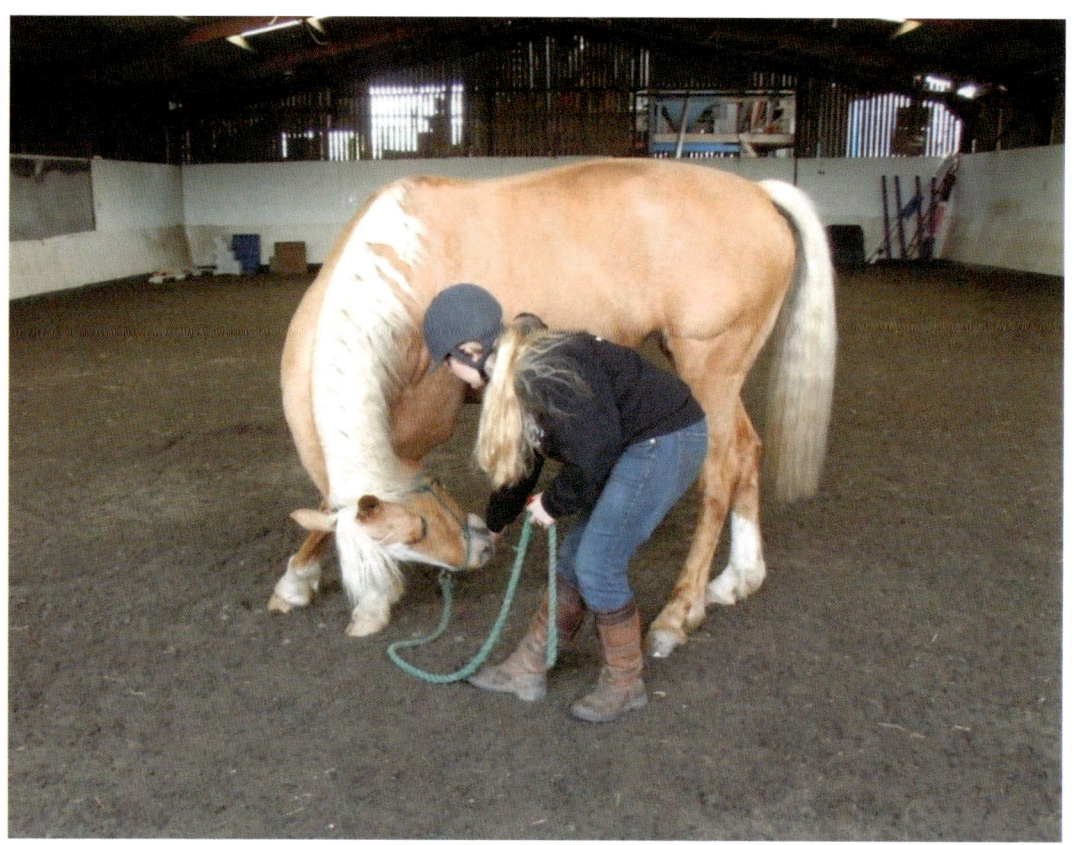

Lesson 4: Once your horse will cross his legs and drop his nose you are ready to start on the actual bow. Ask your horse to resume the position with nose on the floor and cue for the 'Bow'. Do this by taking a treat in your right hand, holding the clicker and lead rope in your left, and enticing your horse to reach down and back as in the bow. CARE** Do not hold the treat too far back at first, as your horse may lose his balance or strain himself when not used to this movement. Click and reward as the horse reaches position, and make a big fuss of him. Repeat these two or three times, for the first few sessions.

Lesson 5: Practice Lesson 4, gradually increasing the distance your horse bows his head. The further he goes the further he will have to shift his weight to his back legs and brace with the front. As they are crossed he will need some time to find his balance and coordination and build up the muscle required, so take care to do this gradually. Once your horse has mastered the Queen's Bow, technique you should now practise holding the position. This can be done by very slowly lengthening the time your horse stays in position before you click and reward. Once in position ask him to 'stay! stay! stay!', until he hears the click for his treat. Increase this by a matter of seconds in each practice and he'll soon be performing like the star he is!

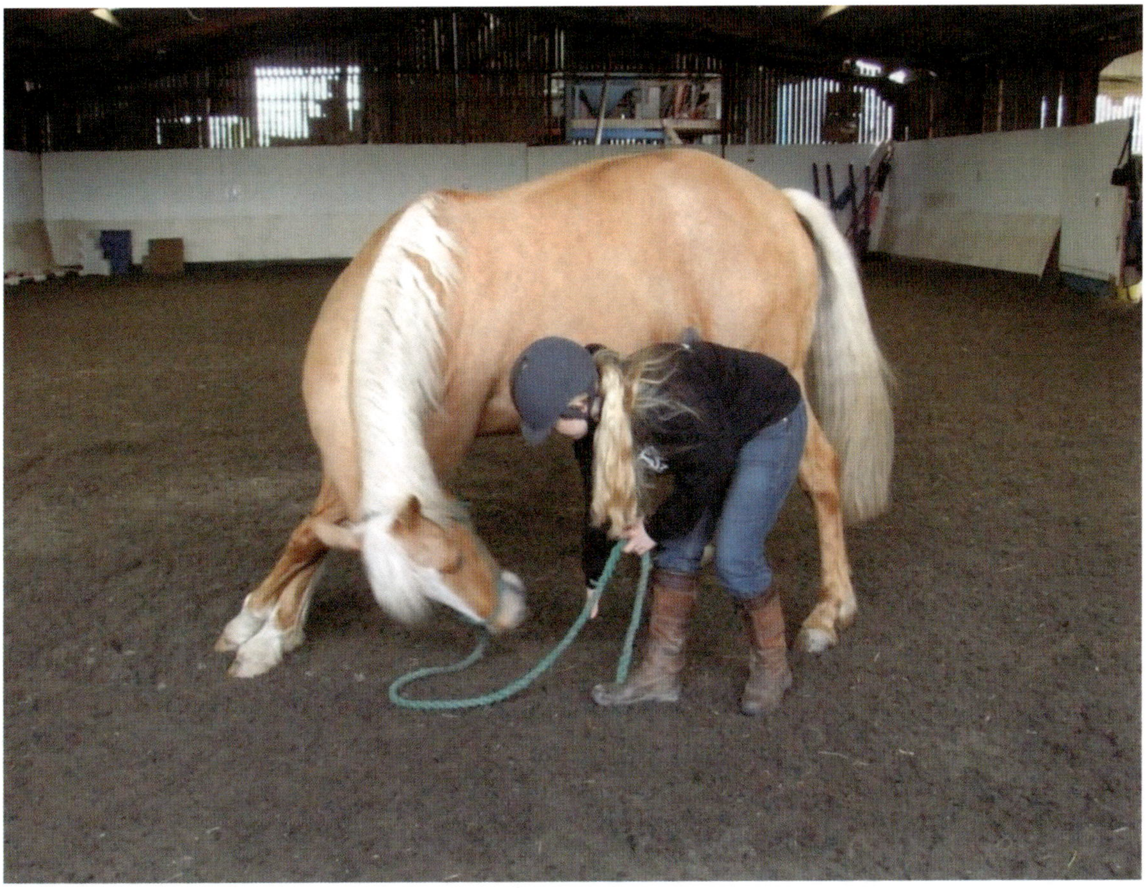

Chapter 6: Pedestal Work

Now that your horse has got this far it is time, to move things up a step, so to speak!

Anyone who is familiar with animal acts under the circus big top will have seen a horse or an elephant performing on top of a specially constructed box called a pedestal.

Box work tests your horses trust in you, so please make sure that you only use a pedestal up to the job and your horse's weight. It must not tip over, and have a non-slip surface to ensure your horse won't be injured and feels safe.

To become successful on the pedestal your horse needs to become fully aware of their body and conscious of what their back end is doing as well as the front. Balance and co ordination is vital so the horse has to be attentive and listen to your instructions whilst getting to grips with a new view of the world! Suddenly they find themselves much taller! Most horses enjoy this and will repeatedly return to the box themselves for fun.

The following exercises have many benefits. Firstly and most importantly, sympathetic schooling on a pedestal will promote courage in the most timid of creatures and will focus scatty animals that have trouble concentrating. As your horse progresses, their poise and dexterity levels improve, becoming more confident in them-selves, and trusting of you. Any nervous stress or tension should disappear, and you will find your horse is more likely to investigate new sites and objects that they would have once run away from, as it could turn out to be their next cool toy!

Once a horse has learned to step up on a box he will voluntarily do it again and again without being asked. Your horse has a new view on the world and the experience of looking down on the rest of his friends and trainer is obviously very appealing. Fern absolutely adores her box and will spend ages up there watching the world go by if allowed.

Introducing the Box

To most onlookers this trick can appear to be pretty simple. If you are asking: 'How hard can it be to get a horse to walk up and stand on a box?' Well it depends on the horse. If you are lucky enough to have a horse with a laid back nature it can be that simple. However most horses will need to accustom themselves to this new equipment, learn to trust the box, listen closely to your instructions, conquer their fears, and improve their balance and coordination. In addition, the smaller the box the better their balance and coordination has to be.

Tools Required: - Head Collar, Long Lead Rope, Pedestal, Protective Boots or Bandages, Treats, A trusted and enthusiastic assistant, Purpose made pedestal, strong enough to safely and easily take your horses weight.

Mounting the Pedestal

Lesson 1:- Start by dressing your horse in head collar, lead rope, protective leg wear and ensure you are wearing a hard hat, gloves, and good strong boots. Next, slowly introduce your horse to the box. Let them take their own time to investigate and approach this new object, and reward them as soon as they touch it with a foot or even sniffing and nuzzling it by accident until your horse will happily walk up to and stand next to the box without any concern.

Lesson 2:- Approach the box and reward your horse for standing calmly next to it. Next pick up one of his front legs and try and place it on top of the box. Praise and reward the horse every time he touches the top with a toe even if it doesn't remain there. Soon your horse will link the touching of the box with his foot to the reward and will begin to do it voluntarily

in the hope it will earn another treat. With practise the foot will remain on the box for longer periods as your horse learns a hoof on the box means treats and begins to offer the behaviour.

Lesson 3:- Now your horse is happy to pop one foot up on the box, it's time to work on the other foreleg. In many cases, the horses will be so eager for a treat the second foot will follow automatically. If this doesn't happen, don't worry, repeat step 2 with the opposite leg. In time you will be able to encourage the horse forward with a treat so both legs are in position.

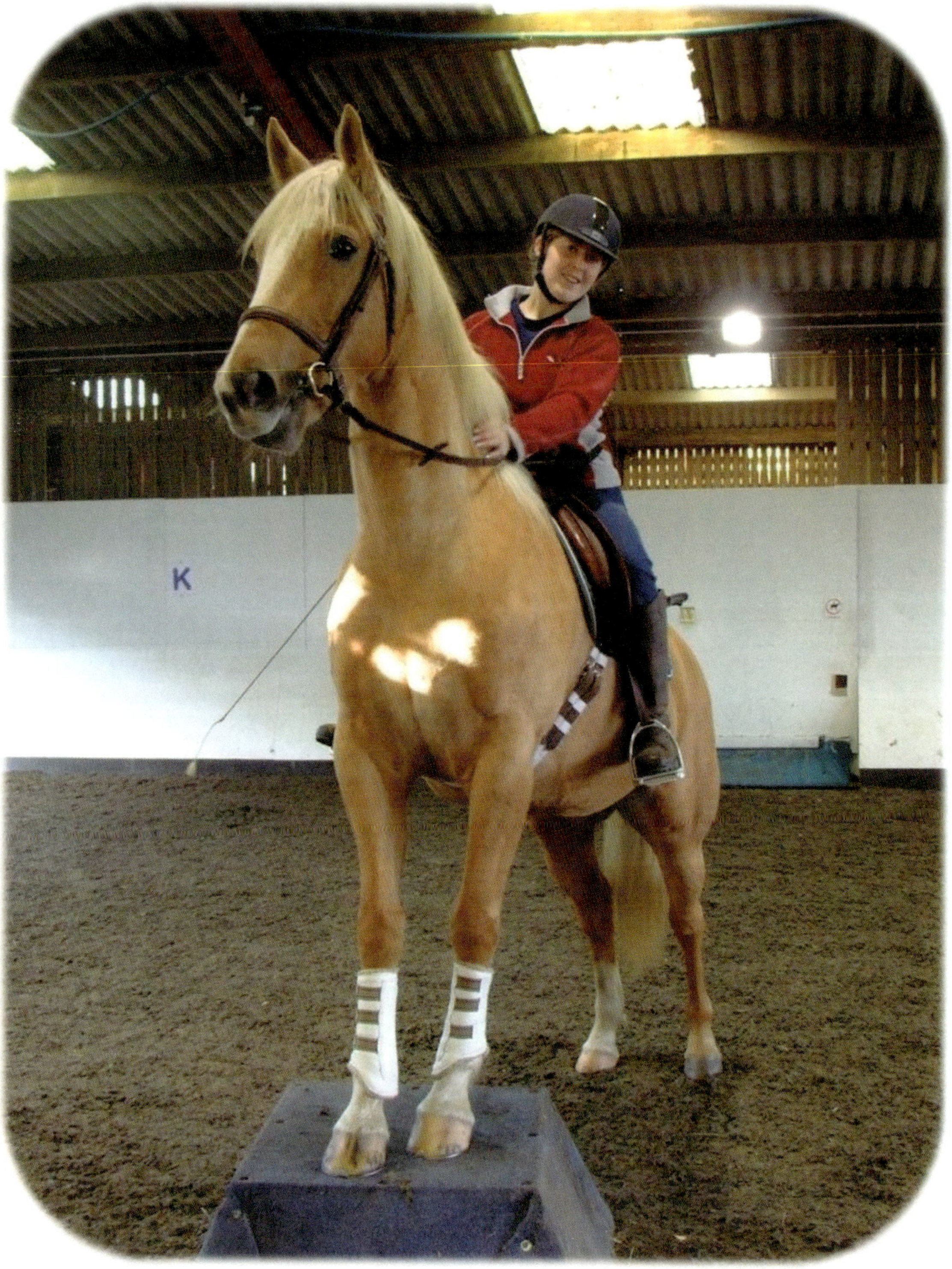

Lesson 4: When your horse is comfortable placing both front feet on the box it's time to concentrate on the rear legs. Horses appear to be less aware of their hind legs, and find their precise placement on a small box very difficult. When asked to move a rear leg the horse's natural instinct is to move a front leg and walk forward, often straight off the box. Indeed some horses can jump right over the box or will plant their front feet and completely refuse to move. For this reason I prefer to go back to the basics and request the horse first to walk over a flat plywood board.

Request your horse to place his front feet on the board, and click and reward as soon as he obliges. Next, ask your horse to lift his left and right legs alternatively. As he lifts each leg gently encourage the foot to land a bit further forward by applying a little pressure on the lead, clicking and rewarding if you make any forward progress.

By asking you horse to concentrate on the left and right leg trick, you will prevent his mind from wandering and worrying about freezing on the spot or jumping forward. Slowly, with great patience, you will eventually be able to lead him forward straight over the board. Click and reward very well when that first hind hoof steps onto the board. Continue to practice this until your horse will walk straight over the board without hesitation.

Lesson 5: Next raise the level of the board slightly off the floor and repeat lesson 4. To do this I recommend securing the same board with screws onto a low but strong wooden brick pallet that can easily support up to a tonne in weight and won't tip over. Once your horse has the front legs in position you will need to help him with the placing of his hind legs. Insist that your horse stands still and gently encourage him to raise a hind leg by squeezing the skin on the hock. As the horse picks up a toe, gently guide it onto the pallet, as soon as it touches click and reward well. Repeat with the other hind leg. Keep practising until he can easily place all four feet on the platform. If your horse moves his front feet at any point, stop, firmly tell him no and correct him, starting again from the beginning.

Lesson 6: Next you want to get the horse to stop and think, with the hind legs still on the box. Ask for the front feet up, and reward. Lead forward and, as soon as a back toe touches the box, stop your horse and reward. Keep practising until you can stop your horse for a reward at any point rather than having him rush over the box.

Lesson 7: A trusted helper at this point will come in very useful. Request your horse to place the front feet on the box again. Ask you assistant to hold your horse's head and front end still, with a treat or two in the pocket to keep the horse's attention. Moving to the flanks, you can then concentrate on tapping the hind leg with the schooling whip until the horse lifts the leg just off the floor. Click and reward well, you are trying to make the horse think about lifting the leg. He will find it quite challenging whilst he is unbalanced with his fore legs on a higher level. Repeat, but ask your assistant to get your horse to drop his head which shifts more weight to the front. Then you can practise raising the hind leg and holding the hoof in your hand, click and reward.

Lesson 8: Repeat lessons 6, but this time with front legs on the box, ask your assistant to drop your horse's nose once again. This time tap the hind leg to raise it with the schooling whip and take the hoof by the hand. Pull the leg forward, and try and place the toe on the box. As soon as it touches click, and ask your assistant to reward. Your horse more than likely will try and reverse off the box, or pull his leg away. If this happens reposition the front legs, and ask for the foot to be placed on the box again. Repeat this, clicking and rewarding, until the horse leaves the foot in place waiting for his treat, and is comfortable holding that position for short periods.

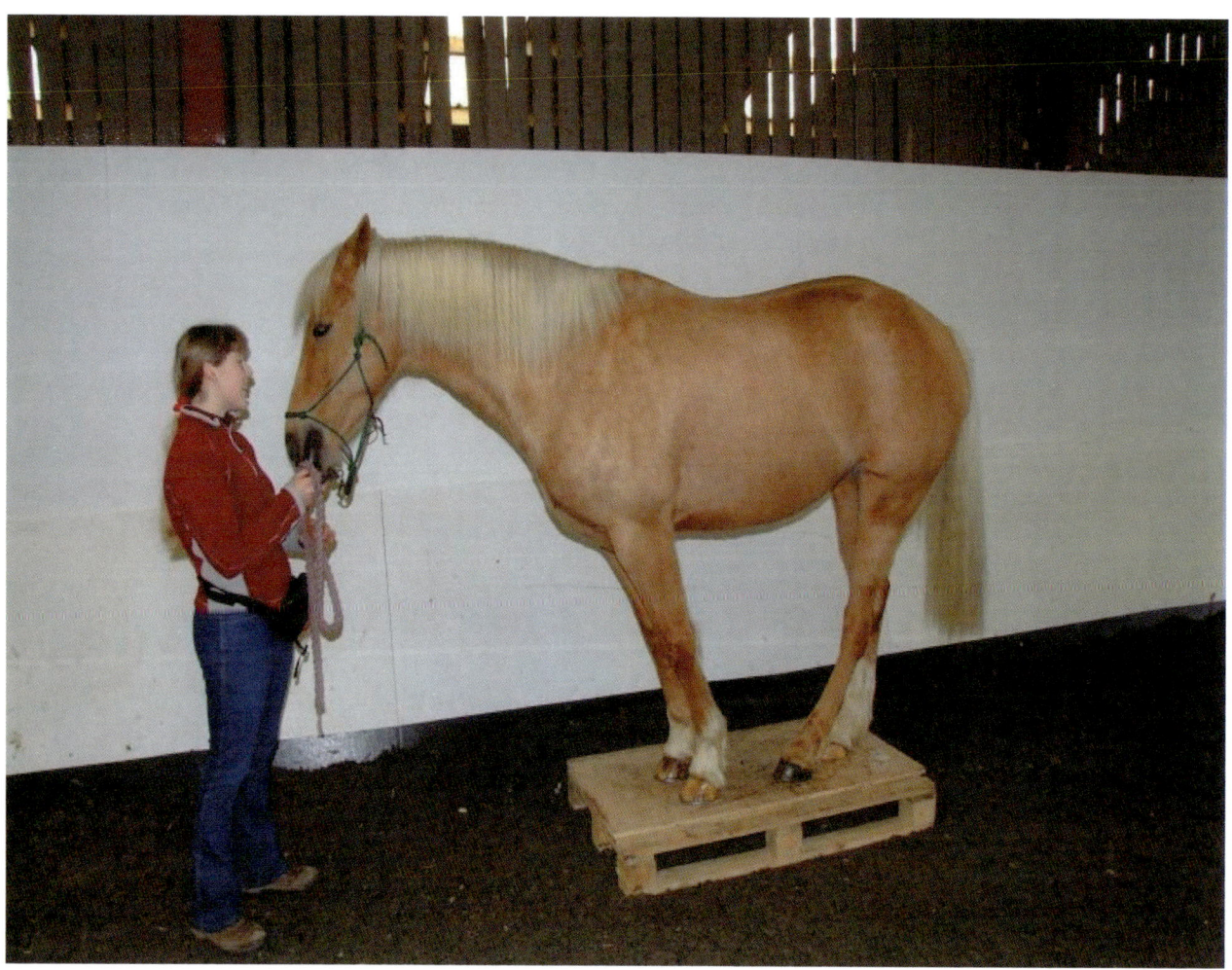

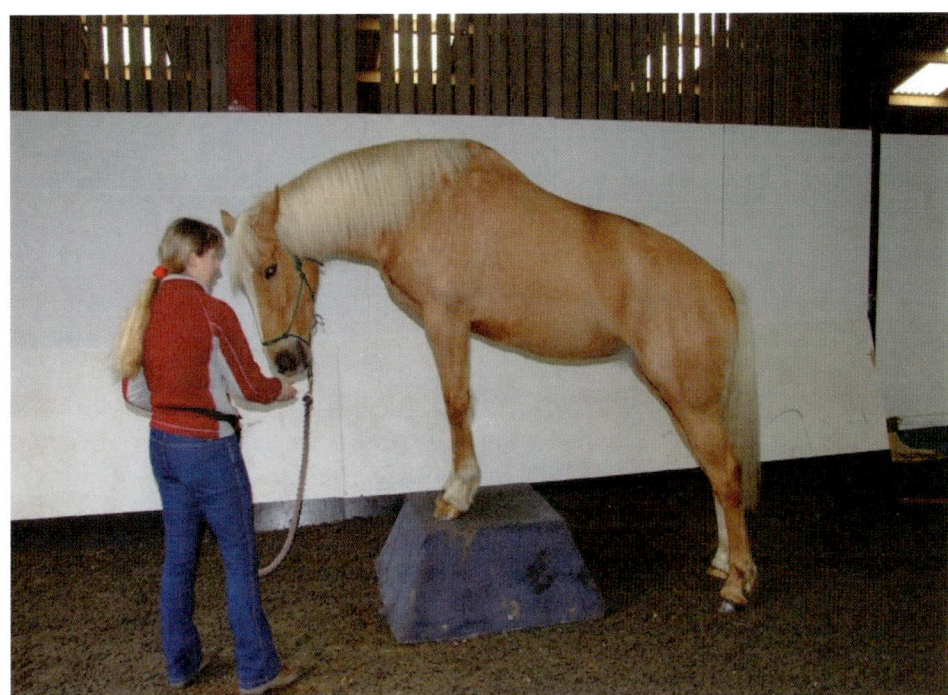
Position front feet to leave plenty of room for the hind legs

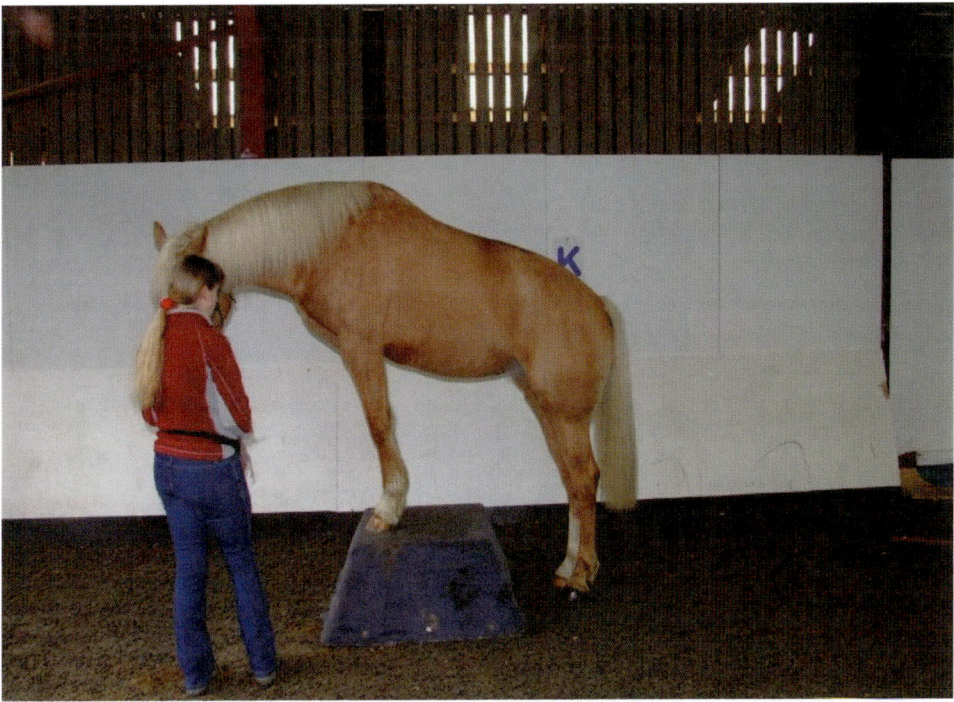
Request that the hind legs move closer to the pedestal

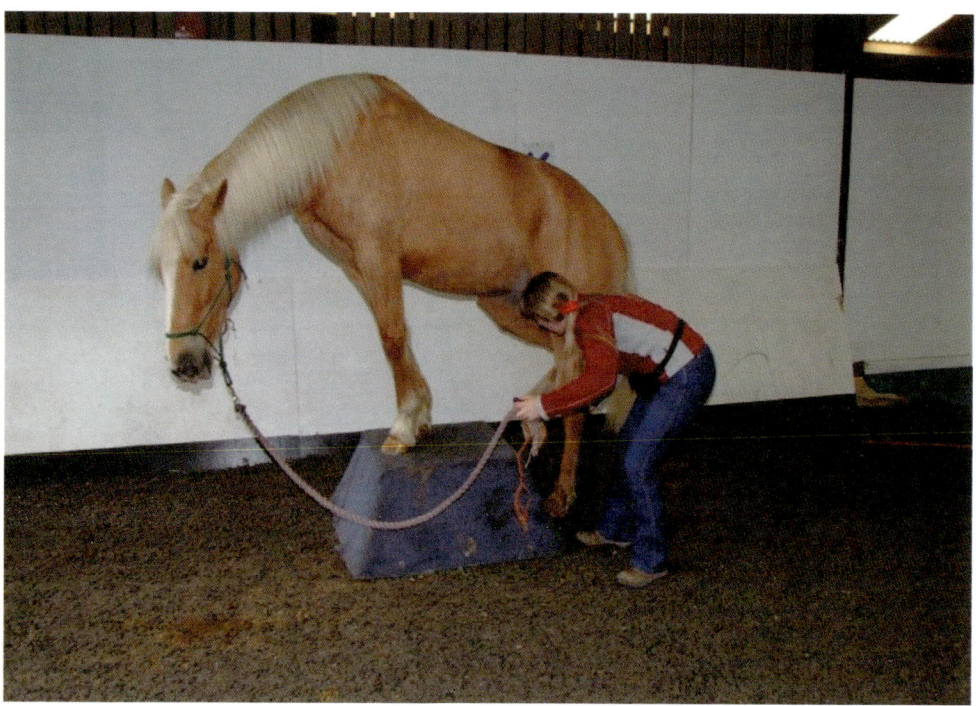

Gently help place a hind leg on the box

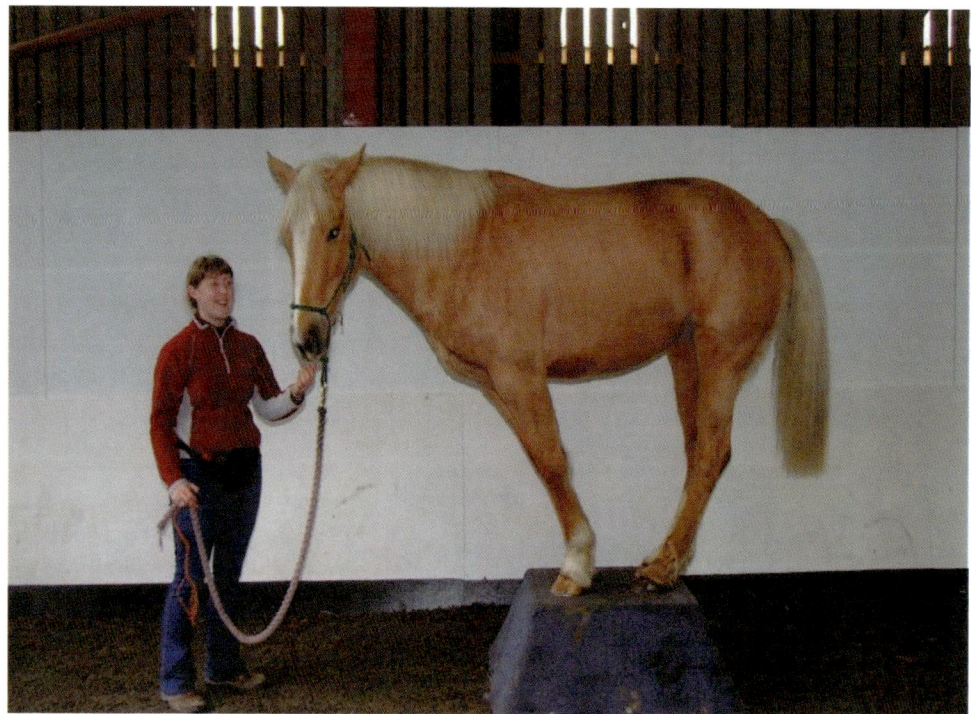

When your horse is happy encourage the last leg to follow and hold that pose!

Pirouette on the Box

This is another combination trick and has two separate variations. The first, of course, is with the front feet on the box. Your horse is asked to do a turn on the forehand with the rear legs circling the pedestal on the ground.

The second variation is 'bottoms up' the hind quarters only remain on the box while you ask your horse to do a turn on the haunches with the forelegs circling the pedestal. Both are a test for your horse's balance and coordination.

Tools Required: Head Collar, Lead Rope, Pedestal, Clicker, Treats

Lesson 1: Dress your horse in head collar and lead rope and ask your horse to mount the pedestal with both front legs. Stand level with your horse's shoulder with the lead in your left hand and the clicker and whip in your right. Now ask your horse to move his quarters away from you. Click and reward on any effort to move in the desired direction without stepping off the box. You can encourage the horse to move the hind legs round by gently pulling the nose round towards you with the lead. Do this in tiny increments at first so your horse can keep his balance on the box.

Lesson 2: Repeat lesson 1, until your horse can move his hind legs 360 degrees around the box with the lightest of touches with the whip on the point of hip. Click, reward and praise well once you have completed one rotation. Finally, you are aiming to just gesture toward the hip with the whip to cue the rotation.

Variation: Bottoms Up

Ask the horse to mount the box with all four feet. Then ask him to dismount the box slowly so his hind feet remain 'Bottoms Up'. This may take a little practice as the horse will be in a rush to hop off the box.

With the hind legs in the correct position cue the front legs to cross towards you and gently pull the head around until you complete a 360degree turn on the haunches.

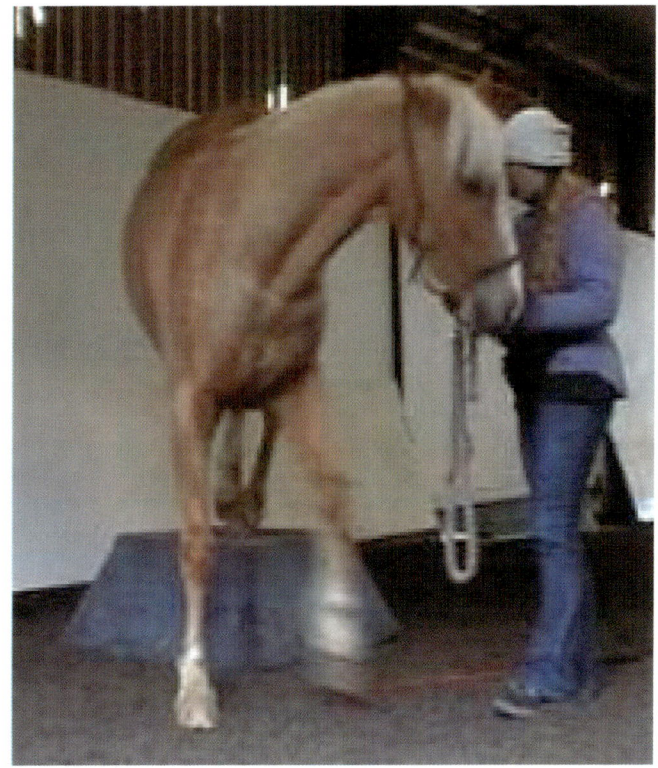

Curtsy Bow on the Box

122

In theory if you have mastered the Curtsy Bow on the floor and can get your horse's front legs on the box, then this should be easy. However you must consider that your horse's centre of gravity is different whilst his front legs are up on the box compared to what it would be standing flat on the floor, and thus will take a little while to find his balance and confidence. He also has to consider moving and positioning his front legs farther apart, which will grow with experience and practice.

I highly recommend that this lesson is practised only after exercise. At this angle, your horse can accidentally strain something if he is not sufficiently warmed up first. I also suggest stretching exercises on the front legs, even if it is only practising the 'Jambette' (see page 125) beforehand, this will warm and stretch the muscles and tendons in the front legs and back.

Tools Required:
Head Collar, Lead Rope, Pedestal, Clicker, Treats

Lesson 1: Refresh your horse with mounting the pedestal with his front legs and click and praise him well for it.

Lesson 2: Practise also the Curtsy Bow on the flat ground ensuring your horse knows how to move and position his forelegs well. You need to get the horse to swing as far back as possible. This will, overtime, strengthen the back and forelegs. Be careful not to do this too much, too soon, but build on it gradually. This is very important, as the additional height of the pedestal will put added strain to the front limbs and back.

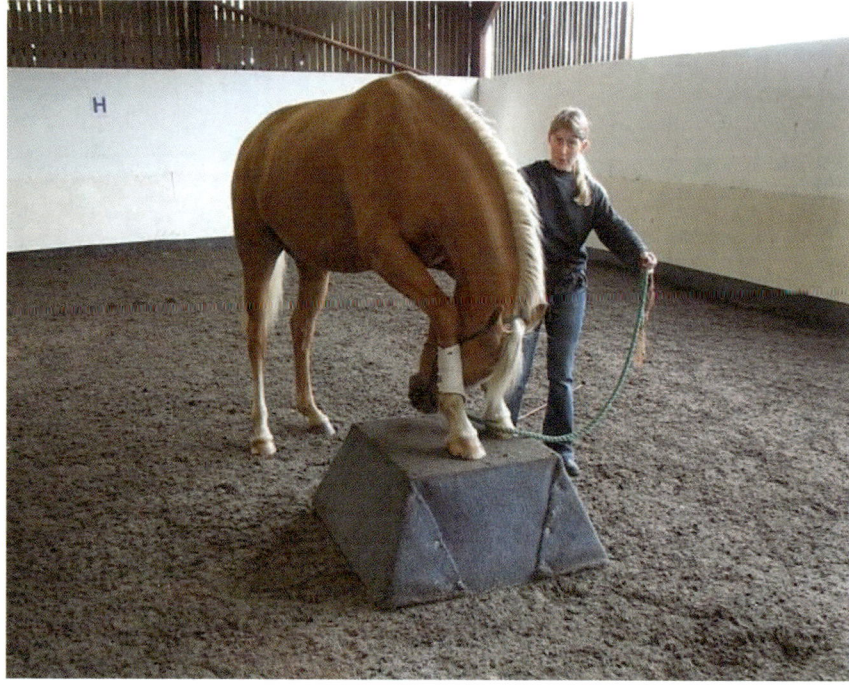

Lesson 3:- Pay particular attention to the placing of your horse's feet on the box. The feet must be flat on the box and closer to the edge than normal. You must also get them far enough apart to assist your horse to balance correctly, leaving plenty of room for your horse's head.

Chapter 7: Fancy Footwork! The Finale

123

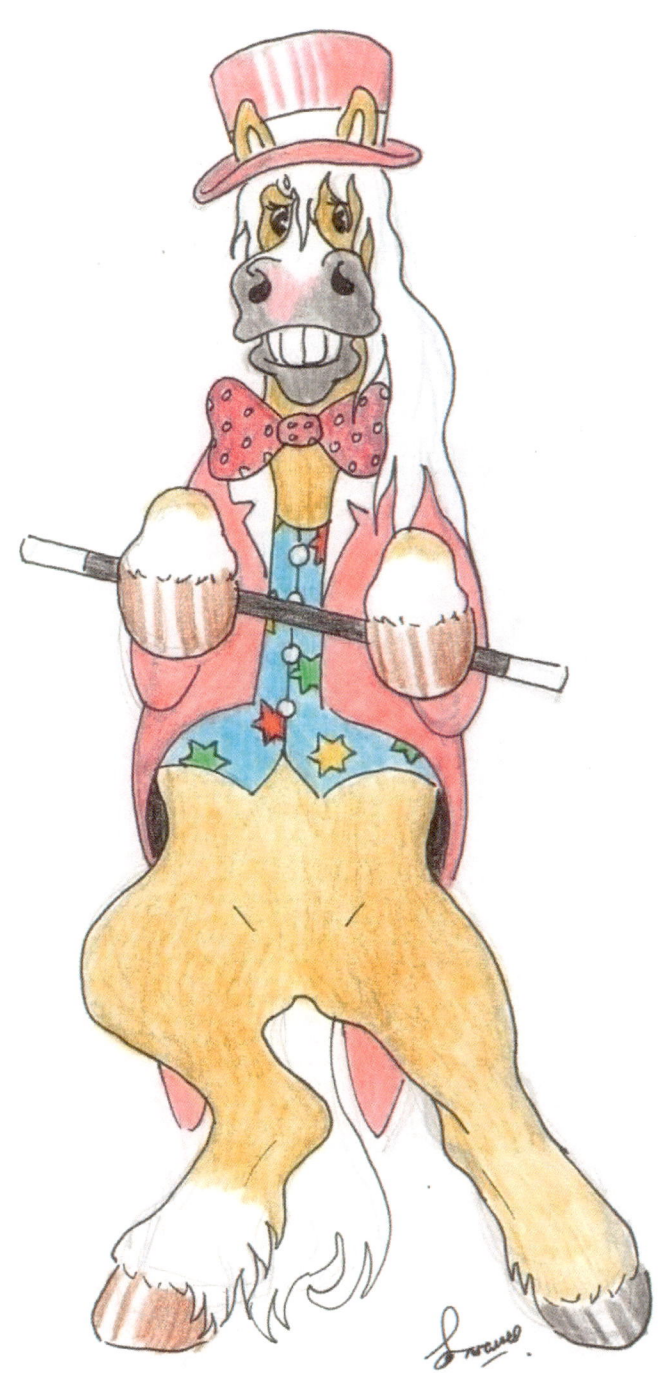

There are many movements we can class as fancy foot work, that leave the average horse owner in admiration and awe of those who achieve them. Movements such as the Spanish Walk or Trot look so impressive you would imagine they are a testament to the trainer's skill. The truth is anyone can do it when shown how!

These lessons lead to a horse that is so in tune with their handler, they can almost dance together, a true test of partnership and communication.

The following lessons will improve your horse's strength, suppleness, attentiveness and coordination. Many are so testing or physically demanding that not all horses can achieve the ideal and hence such movements don't make it into the competition world. After all, not all humans are cut out for a local barn dance let alone for the National Ballet!

Before beginning this section please take an honest look at your training ability, and ask yourself: do you want to teach these movements, and once taught will you be able to confidently control them? If you are inexperienced, or do not have complete trust and obedience from your horse at this stage, please don't go any further. The horse must understand that such activities must only be performed on cue and if you have problems communicating this in your training then it is unwise to proceed without professional help.

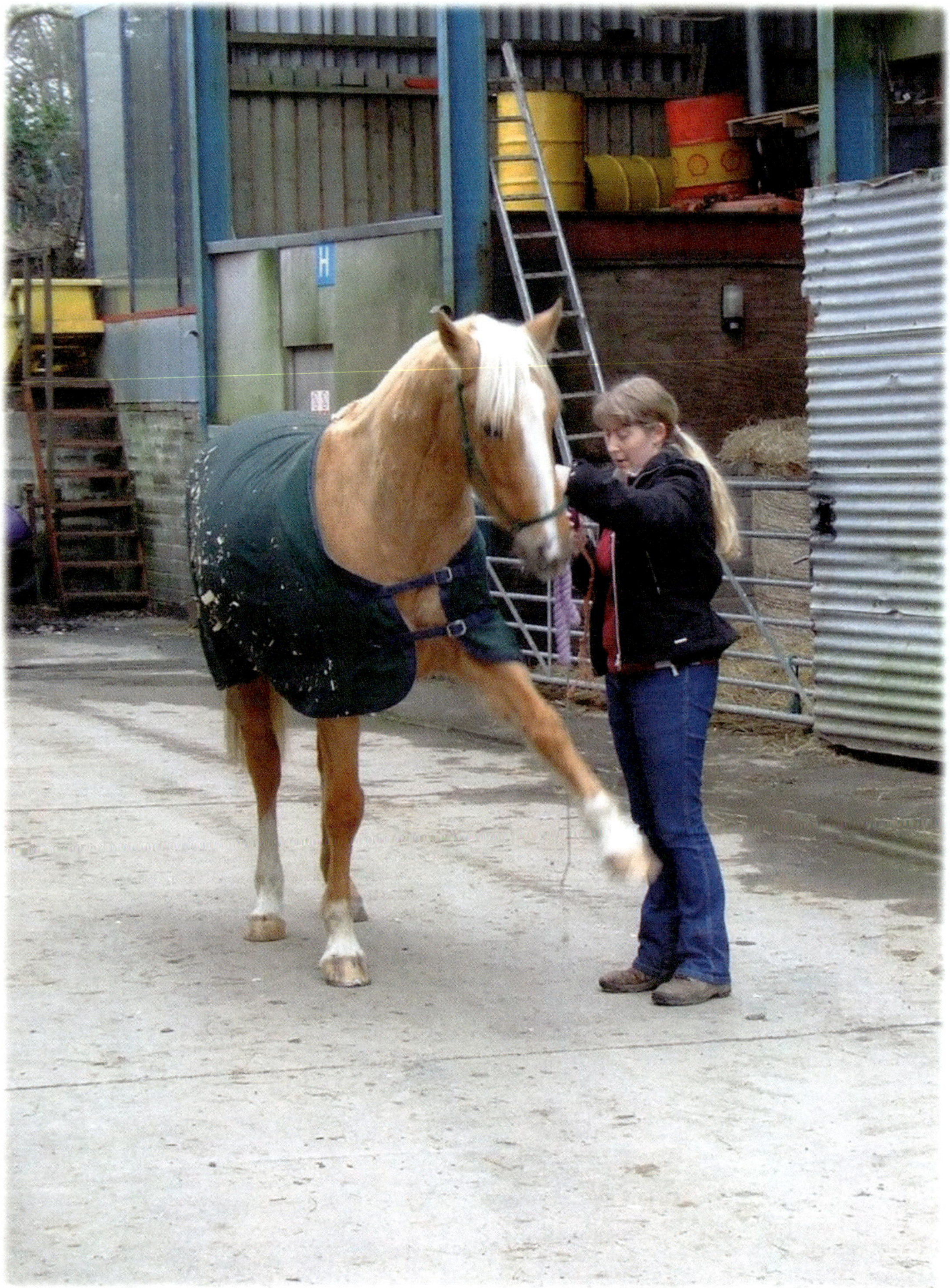

124

Spanish Walk

Now for some fancy footwork! The Spanish Walk is a beautiful, impressive high stepping marching movement. Most commonly seen and admired in the Spanish training schools where breeds known for a high stepping leg carriage such as the Lipizzaner and Andalusian perform this breathtakingly expressive walk. It can be practised in hand, under saddle, or by long rein, and taught to any horse. It encourages gymnastic stretching, a high degree of coordination, whilst also developing a fantastic carriage through the effort it entails.

In an earlier chapter we learnt how to encourage the horse to offer a left or right leg on request. Taking that training one step further, we can develop the impressive Spanish Walk.

Tools Required: Halter, Bridle, Saddle, and Lead rope, Schooling Whip, Clicker and Treats

Working in Hand

Lesson 1:- Dress your horse in head collar and lead rope, and start by practising the 'Left & Right Trick' (See page 64)

Lesson 2:- Once the horse can pick up left and right legs on cue, you can begin to refine the movements and mould them into the Classical Spanish Walk. Standing at the near side shoulder, try asking for a leg using the original commands of 'right' or 'left please'

Follow the whip cue up with the word 'High!', whilst raising the level of your horse's head. The higher the head, the lighter the forehand, and thus the horse can raise the legs higher into the extended leg position otherwise known as the 'Jambette'. As with every other trick, click, praise, and reward for every effort made. It should also be noted that the higher the whip is used on the front leg, often the higher the 'Jambette'. Withholding the reward and praise and persistently asking for a higher leg strike can also result in an exaggerated effort from the horse; this should be rewarded immediately and praised well if achieved.

Lesson 3: Keep practising lesson 2 until you can get alternate leg extensions whilst standing to one side of your horse. Once achieved, start to practise forward movement between each step. To do this

ask for the leg rise, and then gently encourage the horse to step forward when putting the foot back on the ground. Again, alternate and reward for each good effort. It will take some time for the horse to find his coordination and to be able to step forward with confidence. You may, at this early stage, notice the horse prefers to stretch with one fore leg and stomp with the other. Don't scold for this it is purely part of the learning process, the horse can be right or left footed and will stomp with the foot he is less comfortable with until he is well practised at it. Whilst concentrating on the forehand the horse will undoubtedly lack forward impulsion and the hind legs will appear to get left behind. This will resolve itself naturally with practise once the horse has established a free flowing rhythm in the movement.

Repeating the exercise frequently with the promise of reward should result in the movement being performed with heightened enthusiasm and expression.

Lesson 4:- Continue to practise stage 3 with minimum use of the whip and use of the verbal commands, 'left high' and 'right high'. Encourage more forward momentum until good impulsion is also observed in the hind legs.

Working under Saddle

Lesson 5:- Once your horse has mastered the movement on the ground, the Spanish walk can easily be taught under saddle. After your horse has been warmed up, collect your reins whilst holding a schooling whip in each hand and ask your horse to stand still and square. The command to raise each leg should be followed by a light squeeze on the corresponding rein, following up with the whip only if necessary, and a tap with your toe behind the horse's elbow. Click, reward and treat for every try. Practise frequently for short periods and alternate between legs.

Lesson 6:- Practise lesson 5 as often as possible. At this stage, your horse may get slightly confused and may move in a variety of directions. To avoid this it may be best to position yourself in the corner of the arena or next to a wall. Should your horse move off, gently correct and insist that the horse is standing quietly before trying the aids again. You require your horse's full, calm, attention so that he concentrates on the aids and does not get confused with you trying to correct or control. This may take a little patience, as your horse does not have your body language to read as on the ground. Your may find it helpful to have a helper on the ground to back up your aids with the whip should you horse find it difficult to understand.

Lesson 7:- Keep practicing and alternating the leg raises. A whip held in each hand will be useful during the early stages to back up the rein and leg aid on each side. Once your horse is comfortable with the aids, you can start applying a leg squeeze to encourage the horse forward between each raise. You must practise the timing of the squeeze just after the horse has extended the foreleg so it is also driven forward; just before the foot hits the floor the opposite aids can be applied to raise the alternate leg. This takes a lot of practice not only for your horse, but for your own timing and coordination. Relax and have fun, remain patient. To perform this properly you must also work on your horse's general collection and outline. A horse in correct outline will have more weight on the hind quarters, enabling him to lift his front carriage and be more expressive with the height of the front leg movement. To begin with, concentrate on the movement, refinement, and your presentation will naturally follow when you horse understands and has mastered the coordination needed

Lesson 8:- Be clear whilst practising, and apply aids in sequence until the horse learns to start the Spanish walk just from you squeezing the reins. Work on a system of squeeze rein and verbal cue, if there is no reaction, follow with a tap with your toe behind the elbow, if there is still no reaction, then, follow with the whip tap on the appropriate shoulder. Soon you horse will learn to react to the rein aid, and the verbal cue, toe tapping and whip can be dispensed with. Reward and click often for every bit of progress made.

> **Training Tip:-** Only reward your horse for a front leg lift when you have cued the movement, rewarding a horse for offering this without being asked can lead to a habitual stiker which is not only disrespectful but can be dangerous. You might also find it useful to practice the work under saddle in front of a mirror or somewhere you can see your shadow, as it is easier to tell when your horse has lifted the leg correctly.

DID YOU KNOW? A variation of the traditional Spanish Walk is the 'Polka'. It takes a little more thought, control, obedience, and coordination, from your horse, but this is an ideal exercise to test how attentive and well trained your horse is at Spanish Walk. The Polka consists of 1 high step, followed by two normal at walk, followed by another high step, and so on. The sequence is **Left high**, two three, **Right high**, two, three etc.

Note: Once the Spanish Walk has been mastered, the Spanish trot will often be offered completely naturally by the horse. Placing the horse in a collected trot and applying the same rein and leg aids as per Spanish Walk will trigger the high leg action. This will need to be practised in order to perfect coordination, tempo, and collection. But is amazing to watch and well worth the further effort.

The Spanish Trot is similar to passage but the front legs are extended when raised rather than bent at the knee. Ideally, we are aiming for the hind legs to be drawn further under the body taking on more weight with a powerful spring like action, whilst the forehand is lightened and the upper forelegs rise to the horizontal level.

The correct execution of the movement depends greatly on the natural talent of the horse, requiring balance, noble self carriage, confirmation, and elegance, like that of a dancer. Not every human can dance gracefully and the horse is no different, some are better dancers than others!

129

The Rear & Collected Variations

Hi Ho Silver! This is a spectacular move, and one of the first lessons in the Airs above the Ground! The Rear embodies the sheer power, grace, and baroque beauty of the horse. It was originally taught under saddle for defensive riding on the battlefield. In recent centuries the movement was refined into variations such as Levade and Pesade by the famous riding schools for display and performance purposes.

Taught well and safely it is a fantastic movement to add to your repertoire. However, I cannot emphasise strongly enough how much caution should be taken to ensure that teaching the Rear does not lead to behavioural problems, a defensive act, or evasion. I highly recommend you seek professional assessment and guidance in your training if this is the first time you have worked on this movement. Always ensure that you have complete respect from your horse and that ground handling is well established before you begin. It is also best taught to relatively calm and sensible animals until you have the experience, confidence, and ability, to try this with a feistier horse.

The Rear is usually one of the last tricks taught, simply because it is best to wait until the horse understands the basic communications from earlier tricks, and has the discipline to understand it must only be performed on cue. It is an easy movement to trigger without any preparation. A horse will often Rear due to pain caused in the mouth from novice rider pulling on the reins for example or in self-defence from something alarming. This is why we need to teach a controlled and natural cue that the horse will understand and perform to, whilst preventing dangerous or bad habits from forming through confusing signals.

There are several approaches to teaching this movement, the three easiest I outline here. Please note many of the classical trainers also use a cross-tie system working between two fixed pillars to aid in training. I am assuming this is a facility most people will not have and therefore have not covered it in this book.

Tools required: - Head collar & Lead Rope or Bridle, Whip, Treats, Bandages, or splint & overreach boots for your horse, a hard hat, gloves, strong boots and body protector for you.

Safety Caution: When your horse Rears, take care to stand clear of his front legs and hooves to avoid injury.

Method 1: The Collected A safer option for the novice trainer involves the use of the whip to encourage the horse to raise the forehand. This is a better approach for horses who can strike out with the front legs, as it's not as haphazard.

Lesson 1:- Dress your horse in head collar and long lead and stand in front of your horse. Holding the lead in the left hand and schooling whip in the right. Next, begin to lightly tap the top of the neck or cheek close to the throat latch area whilst giving the verbal cue 'Up'. You are looking for any effort to toss the head upwards. At the slightest try stop, praise and reward the horse well. Repeat several times rewarding for any effort to toss the head.

Lesson 2:- Repeat lesson 1, gradually asking for more head toss before offering the reward. Tap a little harder or play with the general area of the taps until you find the area that gives you the best reaction. Watch for the front feet leaving the ground at all. The first effort will usually be a small bunny hop combined with the head toss. Depending on the sensitivity of your horse this can happen immediately or take quite some time to develop. As soon as this occurs go overboard with the praise, reward and end the lesson.

Lesson 3:- Repeat the training sessions until your horse is offering the little 'hop' on cue. Reward as you go. Once it is well established, start with-holding the treats and asking for more height, you should note asking your horse to perform the move several times in a row at this stage without reward should encourage the horse to try harder and hop higher. Think of it as shouting, the horse will think you did not hear them the first time and shout a little harder for the attention and reward by putting more effort into his next try.

Lesson 4:- As the hop becomes more of a Rear, there is a danger of the front legs lashing out and catching the rope. Should this happen quietly stop and calmly untangle the legs and start again so as not to alarm your horse. Any fuss on your part can encourage panic in your horse, as he is looking to you for reassurance. Continue the lesson until the Rear is well established and you only have to gesture upwards with the whip to cue the Rear. Your horse will learn to read your gesture, and predict the tap on the neck and react accordingly. Eventually raising the whip above your head will be recognised as the cue for the Rear.

Left: *The Pesade is a controlled variation of the Rear. The horses back should form an angle of up to 45 degrees to the ground with the front legs drawn in together. The closer the nose is to 45 degrees to the back the neater the position of the front legs in Rear*

Method 2: Natural Play

This approach is fast and draws on a young or energetic horse's willingness to play. Great care should be taken with regards to safety. You must be confident in your ability to reward and control the behaviour to obtain a safe and controlled Rear on cue, rather than a pushy excitable horse that starts to Rear for attention, naughtiness, or bullying.

Lesson 1:- In an enclosed space, such as a round pen or school, begin to play with your horse by asking him to follow you around. Reward the horse every now and then for his attention. Pick up speed again asking the horse to follow, and cut and dive to change direction encouraging your horse into play mode. Continue taking care to remain cautious of the animal's mounting excitement. Focus on where you are in relation to your horse, as they get more and more boisterous; make use of a whip or rope to flick the horse away to maintain a safe and respectful distance. Continue until the horse starts to Rear and kick up his heels in play.

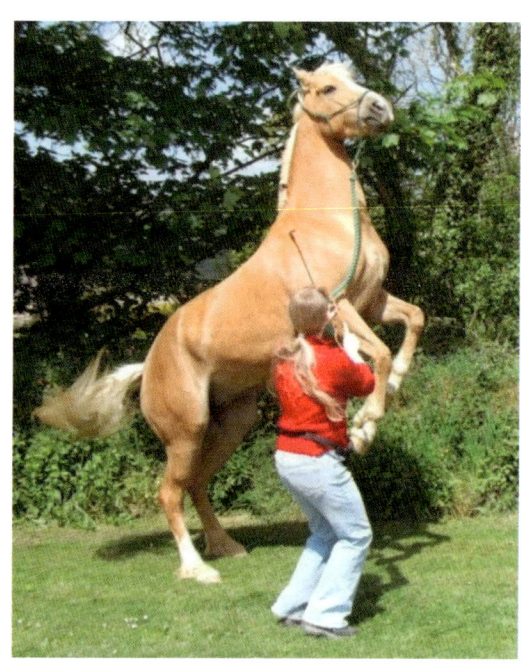

Keep a watchful eye on the behaviour and as soon as the horse front feet leave the floor together, even if it is very slight, click immediately and say the cue 'Up', raising both arms parallel in front of you with a schooling whip in one hand, stop in your tracks and reward well with praise and treats. This should set the cogs turning in your horse's brain as to what they just did that triggered your behaviour!

Lesson 2:- Continue with step one until your horse recognises the word cue 'Up' and the raising of your hands to indicate a Rear. ** VERY IMPORTANT** Be very careful at this stage that as soon as the horse understands what you have been asking, you then only reward a Rear that you have requested with those aids. This is crucial because if you start rewarding when the horse has not been asked they will try to use this action as a bully tactic to get a treat out of you!

Lesson 3:- Now that the horse is responding to your cue, we want to establish a trigger point. To do this, every time the horse Rears to your hand cue, extend the whip and touch the horse in a specific area. I tend to touch the horse lightly on one side of the withers or neck as this can later be used in mounted work. Repeat until the horse recognises this as a cue in itself, and performs primarily to the word cue and touch of whip in this area. NOTE: - From a safety point of view, you now have two different ways to trigger the desired behaviour, and, depending on your situation you can choose the method that works best for you.

Method 3- Targeting

This requires a simple lesson in asking your horse to target an object. For this example we will use a crop.

Lesson 1:- Hold the crop by the lash end in front of your horse and ask him to nuzzle or touch the handle with his nose. As soon as he makes contact with it, praise click and reward him for it. Repeat until he twigs that touching the handle will earn him a treat.

Lesson 2:- Now start moving the whip into different positions asking the horse to seek out the handle and to touch it to claim his reward, this ensures the horse is working a little harder making the effort to follow the crop to earn him his treat. At the same time his concentration will be increasing on following and touching the handle. Continue to click praise and reward when he gets it right.

Lesson 3:- Now that your horse understands and is making the effort to follow the crop, you need to start raising it in the air above his head. Not too high at first! Just high enough to ensure he is stretching to reach it. Once again reward and praise for every effort.

Lesson 4:- Finally you are at the stage where you need to hold the crop just out of reach of your horse's nose. You need to tease him with it until he tries to hop to reach it! At the very slightest sign of a little hop go mad with the clicking, praise and reward. This is the first sign of your horse attempting a rear. Continue practising and raising the crop in order to increase the height and size of the Rears.

Lesson 5:- Gradually increasing the height and time the crop is in the air will improve the Rear and can eventually if practised well, lead to your horse holding the Rear and possibly learning to walk on the hind legs.

Transferral of Cues to the Saddle

Once the Rear can be cued from the ground using the whip, you may wish to continue the training in the saddle and refine it to different levels of height, style, and collection. This movement must only be attempted under saddle if the rider has a fully independent seat and hands. If in any doubt of your abilities do not attempt this.

Lesson 1:- Stand at your horse's side, level with the saddle, and facing towards the horse's head. Gather the reins in the hand nearest to your horse and hold them centred over the pommel of your saddle, hold your schooling whip in the opposite hand. With a relaxed contact, gently lift your reins in an upward movement whilst saying the verbal cue 'Up', and follow this quickly by raising the whip to the neck as you were doing before. This may take a few attempts as you have changed body position, but as soon as there is the slightest hop with the forelegs, reward and praise well, make a big fuss. You will find the next time you ask you are likely to have the desired reaction straight away. Reward well. End the day's lesson at this stage.

Lesson 2:- Now your horse has had a chance to think over the last lesson, start the next one on the ground and refresh his memory by testing him on lesson 1 again. If the correct response is still there, you are okay to climb into the saddle. Begin working on the next phase with an assistant on the ground. Sit deep in the saddle, lift the reins gently and slightly upwards, and combine this with the verbal cue 'Up', follow this up again with raising your whip as before to the horse neck at the same point your horse has become accustomed to. If your horse fails to respond to the aids on the first few attempts it is because he does not have your body cues from the ground to read, so repeat the saddle aids and ask your assistant on the ground to immediately follow these with the familiar ground cues. As soon as your horse makes the effort to hop, reward really well.

Lesson 3:- Repeat the training, gradually reducing the need for the ground assistant by using them only as a backup to the mounted aids. Apply the ground aids only if the horse does not react first to the saddle aids. Eventually the assistant and your whip will no longer be needed and the slightest raising of the reins and the word 'up' will cause lift, so you must concentrate on future rein application. Whilst using an assistant, ensure they stand clear of striking front legs. Also ensure the horse does not Rear so high as to lose his balance and fall over, injuring both himself and his rider. Lean forward and keep the reins relaxed, do not attempt this if you don't have an independent secure seat or you may inadvertently pull your horse over backwards.

> **Training Tip:-** To refine the classical movement, and achieve the nice head position and cleanly folded legs it is helpful to work the horse in side reins. The basic rule is the further the horse's nose is tucked in the tidier the leg position will be.

Variations

Levade describes a controlled Rear where the horse's trunk is carried at an angle of 45° or less to the ground whilst the quarters are lowered and hind legs brought further forward underneath the body. This is a physically demanding movement, requiring superb balance and strength in the flanks and torso. The movement is classified as a 'Half Air' and is where the high school training of horses in 'Airs above Ground' generally begins. Pesade is closer to the classic Rear, although physically demanding; it is easier than the Levade as the horse's torso is elevated above 45° to the ground.

Terre Terre originates from the days of the war horse and early Spanish bullfighting. The movement was developed to intimidate opponents on the ancient battle field. In essence, the horse remains in Levade as long as possible and jumps forward repeatedly, with great balance and agility on the back legs. The war horse would then be taught to strike out at the unfortunate enemy with their free front legs.

Rear Leg Walk is normally only seen amazing the crowds under the circus big top. It is achieved by mastering the Rear by teaching the horse to follow a target stick. The trainer places the horse in Rear and encourages the horse to follow the target stick held aloft by the trainer just out of the horse reach. Thus, the horse needs to gain height, balance, and forward movement, in order to touch the target above his head to gain his praise and reward.

Training Tips:- Should the horse Rear too high you can limit the risk of an accident by softening your aids, lean forward to help the balance and release any pressure on the reins. Otherwise, it is possible that you could accidentally pull both of you over backwards. Always be on your guard when handling a horse that has been trained to Rear. Make sure that anyone that might handle or be around your horse is aware of the cue so that an impromptu rear doesn't occur due to a misunderstanding. If this happens do not blame the horse as it was a genuine effort to do as he is told. If however you are convinced that the Rear was not asked for or provoked, do not chastise the horse or reward with attention; ignore to show this behaviour does not gain him reward or attention when not requested.

The Buck Jump

This very impressive movement should be treated with the same respect and approach as the teaching of the Rear. It is more commonly seen performed by advanced training schools, such as the Spanish Riding School in Vienna, simply due to the discipline, control, and power that must be retained by the horse.

Like many of the high school movements, it's based on completely natural behaviour. Historically the buck jump was part of a war horse's defensive training where it was taught to lash out with the back legs on cue at the enemy. These days the buck jump should only be seen for performance purposes and you are more likely to witness this trick performed in hand rather than under saddle. It takes a great deal of skill from both horse and rider to perform this under saddle, partly due to the power needed by the horse, and partly due to the difficulty of comfortably sitting this movement whilst in the saddle.

The Buck Jump can later be combined with a variation of the Rear called 'Courbette' to culminate in the extravagant movement known as the Capriole.

Important Safety Advice: Great care should be taken to ensure the horse understands that this is a behaviour that should only be performed on cue so it does not lead to vices or problems. Before starting this trick, ensure you horse is physically mature and fit enough to proceed, as it will put excessive strain on the muscles of the back and the joints. Do not attempt this with a growing youngster or an elderly animal. This trick may also not be suitable for horses that are already well established nuisance buckers as they are unlikely to understand and it can encourage the misbehaviour. I strongly recommend horses that already buck without cue should be taken back to basics or avoid this trick altogether as there may be physical or psychological problems that need addressing first.

Only perform this in a safe area, away from spectators that may get too close to flying legs. As with the Rear, only reward for this trick when performed on cue. Ensure that your cue is the same on each occasion so your horse does not confuse the request and lash out in error when you least expect it. You don't want a stranger to give your horse a pat on the rump only to end up flying through the air.

Always apply the Buck cue with the whip and whilst standing at your horse's shoulder, never reward for a buck induced by your hand on the flanks or whilst standing in any other position. This can be extremely dangerous, especially to innocent bystanders, handlers, or riders, who may not be familiar with your horse's training.

Tools Required:- Head Collar, Lead Rope, Protective Boots or Bandages for all four legs, Lunging or Driving Whip without the lash (I use an old lunging or driving whip and have snipped off the lash particularly for this purpose), Treats and Clicker.

Lesson 1: Dress your horse in protective boots or bandages, head collar and lead rope. Make sure you are wearing good boots, helmet, and gloves. Hold the horse's head steady by holding the lead rope with your left hand just below the snap. Stand your horse next to a wall or fence and position yourself at your horse's near side shoulder but no further back than the girth of the horse. Hold the whip and clicker in your right hand. Face towards your horse's tail and start gently tapping the croup area (just above the tail).

You will note a lot of tail swishing, this is a reaction to the nuisance tapping and your horse will try and avoid it by attempting to move away from the whip. As you should be blocking any forward and sideways movement, you horse will only have one direction available to shake off the whip and that is by retaliating with a buck. At the first sign of a buck or kick, immediately drop your whip, click, treat and praise well. Then put your horse away to think about the lesson.

Lesson 2: For the next lesson start with a couple of easy tricks your horse is familiar with. When your horse is performing well in a receptive frame of mind, ask for the buck again. As soon as you get the slightest try, click, praise and reward again. Return to some relaxing easy tricks for a few minutes and try for the buck one more time, when you get the try, reward well and end the lesson there.

Lesson 3: Keep practising lesson 2 in this manner. As the horse begins to understand, you will find he will start to react more quickly to the tap and eventually will produce a buck by just gesturing in the direction of your horse's tail with the whip. As the training progresses, the height and effort put into the buck should improve.

Right: The buck jump can be used as a prelude to more advanced work such as the magnificent Courbette and Capriole, You can see clearly from the slow motion sequence shots: the effort, power and gymnastic ability involved in this movement. This agility must be worked on in conjunction with fitness to obtain a horse that would one day be physically capable of attempting the Capriole or similar movements.

Training Tip: If you find your horse is not very sensitive and will not respond to the whip on the croup then cue your horse for a collected trot in hand on the lead. Whilst in trot your horse's brain is in flight mode and will be more receptive to the idea of a buck. Place your horse in trot and tap the croup repetitively whilst moving. As soon as there is the slightest try to buck, click and reward well. Repeat until you can stop the horse and successfully ask for the same thing through the tapping of the whip.

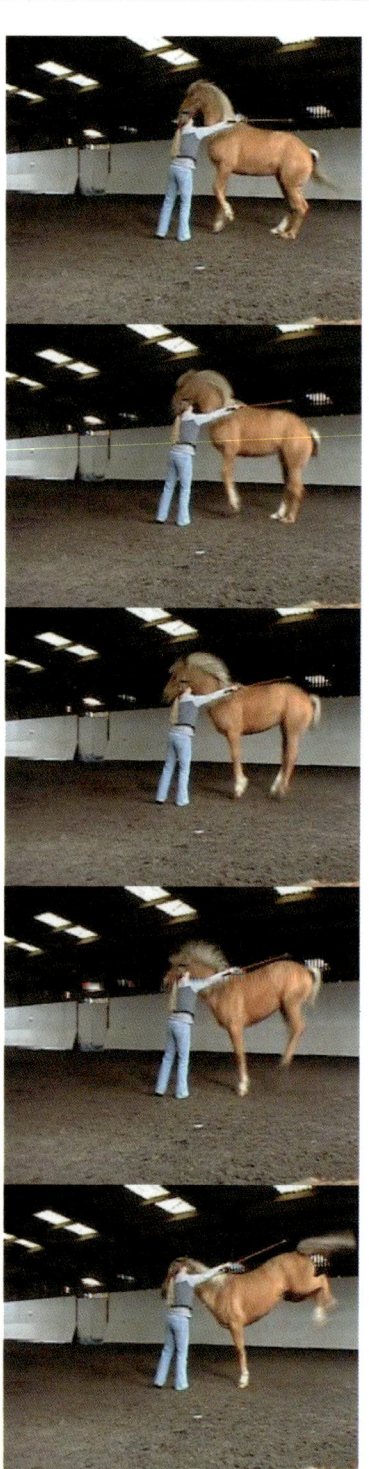

Summary

140

The benefits of trick training your horse are unmistakable. The relationship you have with your horse will in time develop into something that is truly unique. The extra contact, training, and fun times, spent together will build an amazing bond and partnership that is hard to equal.

As you build on your body language and communication skills, your horse will become highly receptive, obedient, fit, relaxed and gymnastically flexible, as well as increasingly intelligent, tuned in to your aids, and completely trusting in you.

This training will last a life time, and the knowledge you gain of horse behaviour will soon become second nature and assist you in handling, teaching, and controlling, virtually any situation with amazing results.

Such training takes commitment, persistence and hard work, it cannot be established overnight. Using kindness and fun is the only way to achieve results; this is often forgotten on those days when things do not go quite right. To get to the top in anything in life you need to start at the beginning and I hope we can guide you in the right direction on your path to equine enlightenment! On your training journey there will be many ups and downs, your patience might wear thin, and you may get close to giving up. You need to stick with it and eventually you will see the light at the end of the tunnel.

Hopefully if you have methodically worked through the lessons in this book you should now have a good understanding of how your horse ticks and using your imagination can come up with even more exciting lessons for the future. You can perhaps now understand that the art of trick training is within reach of everyone with a little time and patience.

On achieving your training goals, the sense of achievement and warm fuzzy feeling towards your beloved horse will be overwhelming. Without doubt trick training is rewarding, exciting and has given my horse and me an amazing, inseparable, almost spiritual connection that I truly wish every horse owner could experience at least once in their life time. If you have a dream, go for it!

Happy Training
Suzanne & Fernoodle

Good luck and have fun everyone!

Appendix 1: How to Make Your Own Rope Halter

Making your own halter takes a little practice but is really simple once you have mastered tying the knots. This step by step guide can save you some money or alternatively you can purchase them at any good saddlers.

You will need: Rope made out of 6mm Marine Double Braided Nylon Rope available from any Yacht Chandlers. This rope is made up of a soft outer braided nylon sleeve over a strong inner nylon core; it is rot resistant and extremely tough and durable. **CARE*** Caution should be taken when the horse is wearing this equipment as it will not break as easily as normal halters in an emergency so should only be worn under supervision . **Also Required:** - Sharp knife or Scissors, box of matches, splicing needle or similar pointed thin utensil.

The following chart gives an approx guide to the amount of rope needed for different sized horses (if uncertain it is best to start with a larger size so you don't' run short of rope half way though making your halter: If you find it is then too big for your horse you can simply undo and start again

Approx Size of Horse-Measure around nose in inches	Length of Rope in Feet
Pony/Young stock Approx 20"	18
Cob Approx 22"	19
Full Approx 24"	21
Ex Full Approx 26"	23

You will now need to master the following knots before you proceed; I suggest you take a few minutes to practice the following techniques before you begin.

The Overhand Knot

This is the easy knot everyone first learns when tying their shoes. The photo below shows the exact route of the rope before it is pulled tight for easy reference.

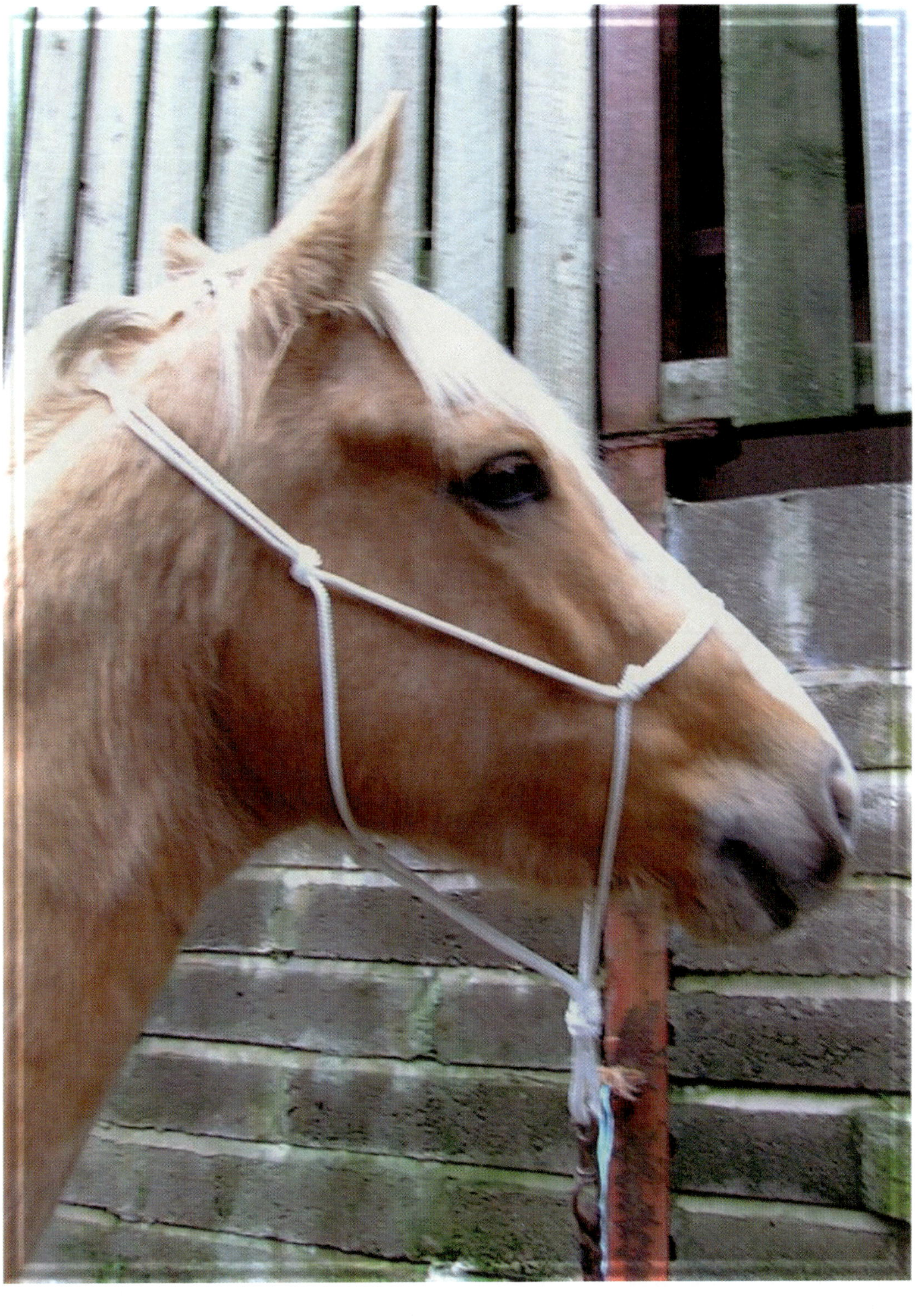

The Double Overhand Knot

A little more difficult to achieve is the double overhand. Starting with the single overhand, a second overhand knot is tied into it resulting in a very tough knot.
Follow the photos below for guidance.

(1) Open up the first overhand knot and slip the second piece of rope through its centre. **(2)** Next loop the rope up and away from you over the 'V' in the first knot and bring the end down and behind the two strands of rope on the left. **(3)** Thread the end through the middle of the first overhand and through the upper loop made in step

two so effectively you are tying a second overhand into the first. **(4)** Pulled tightly you have the Double Overhand which is perfect for pressure training halters as it does not lie flat like some knots.

Constructing Your Rope Halter

Decide which size halter will be appropriate for your horse by first measuring round the nose where a normal Cavesson noseband would sit. Compare your measurement to the table on page 142 for guidance, and cut the appropriate length of rope.

Step 1 to 4: Work from the following diagram and the measurement table. At points A to D tie a simple Overhand knot, but ensure the distance between each knot is measured out correctly.

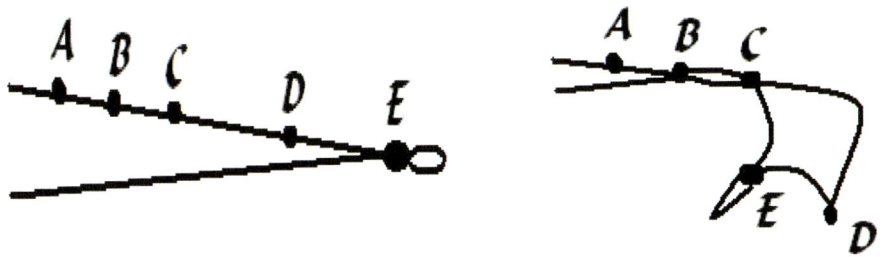

Measurement Table: Distance between knots in inches

Step	Position of Knot	Pony	Cob	Full	XL
1	Start of rope to right Ear A	28	30	32	34
2	Knot A to right nose knot B	7	8	9	10
3	Knot B to left nose knot C	8	9	10	11
4	Knot C to throat latch knot D	29	31	33	35
5	Knot D to tie loop E	8	9	10	11
6	Knot E back to left nose knot C	8	9	10	11
7	Knot C back to right nose knot B	8	9	10	11
8	Knot B back to throat latch knot D	29	31	33	35
9	Knot D to right back to ear knot A	8	9	10	11
10	Knot A to End of rope	28	30	32	34

Step 5: Double the rope over at this point so there is a loop in the rope, then do another overhand to create the side tie loop.

Step 6: After creating the tie loop you will now start to see the collar coming together. From the tie loop 'E' you need to tie your first double overhand by tying back into the left nose knot 'C'.

Step 7: At this point you are going to create the double thick noseband. To do this tie a double overhand at nose knot 'B'. As you do this ensure that both parallel ropes are the same length as this is difficult to correct later on. **Step 8:** From the noseband the next double overhand knot is tied into the throat latch knot 'D'.

Step 9: From the throat latch you now tie a further double overhand into the first ear knot 'A' and you now have a full halter.

Step 10: To make the lead rope loop, lay the head collar out so the two lengths of rope (B to D) & (C to D) are level and together. You now need to make the loop for the lead rope, do this by tying a single overhand knot, leaving two loops approx 4 inches in length.

Step 11: Finally you are left with the two free ends of the rope hanging from the first ear knot 'A'. Combined these will form the poll strap that goes behind the ears and ties to secure the head collar during wear on your horses left cheek.

To join these two pieces neatly you will need to splice the rope. Before doing this I recommend trying the head collar on your horse for size and measure to see where the left hand cheek tie loop and the poll strap meet, add another 10 inches or so to this measurement and you will have the length of rope needed for the poll strap. Trim off any excess rope ensuring both spare ends are equal in length.

Next follow the diagrams to finish joining the straps:-

• Take one of the spare ends and tape the end as flat as possible to a thin pencil, knitting needle or suitable thin and smooth item like a small paintbrush as demonstrated in **diagram A**. Next, a couple of inches from the other spare end, open the weave of the braid by pushing the rope together as per **diagram B**.

• You will note this loosens and enlarges the gaps in the weave large enough to insert a thin tool or pencil. In the loosened section of the weave, insert the end of the pencil or thin object you previously taped the first spare end to as in **diagram C**.

• Thread the object through the weave until it emerges from the end of the rope, **diagram D**. Pull rope all the way through, **diagram E**.

• Finally, remove the item the threaded rope was attached to, and lay the poll strap out straight

Where the spare ends now neatly meet you will notice you are now left with one frayed end. To tidy this up and to link the two pieces permanently hold the frayed end over a lit match and melt the end back to removed the fray, this in turn will bond the two ends neatly and permanently, **diagram F.**

A

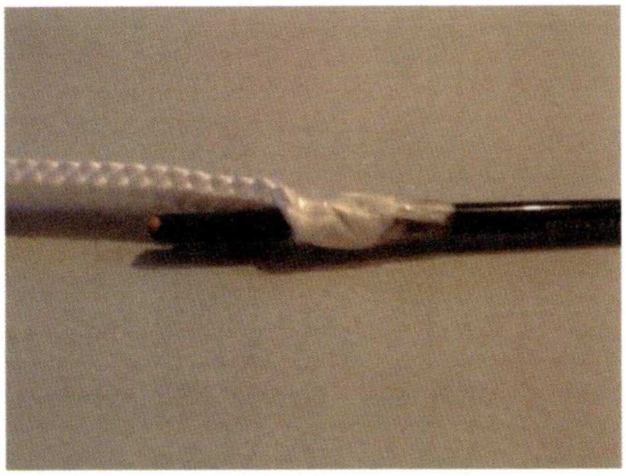

B

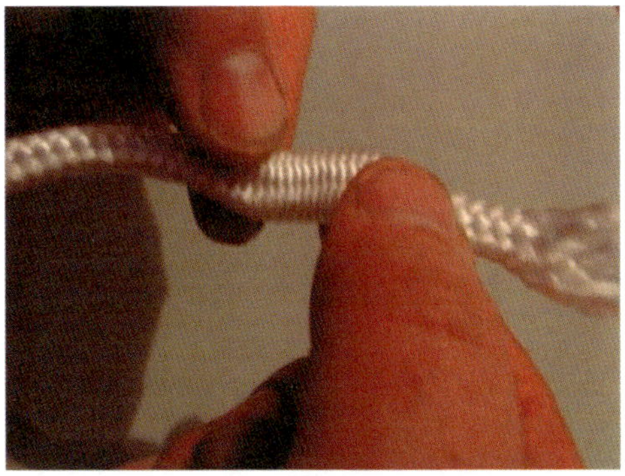

C

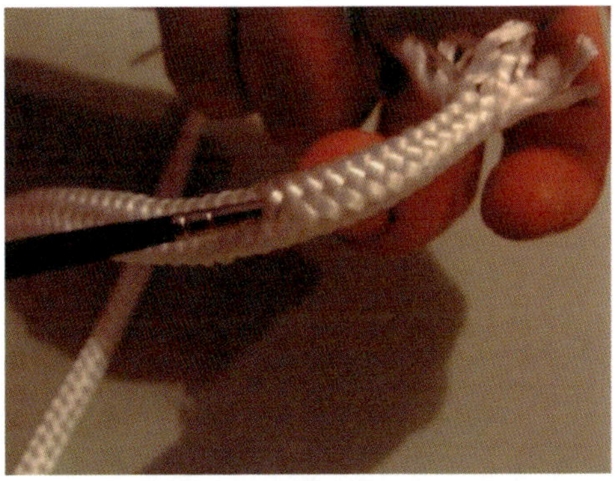

D

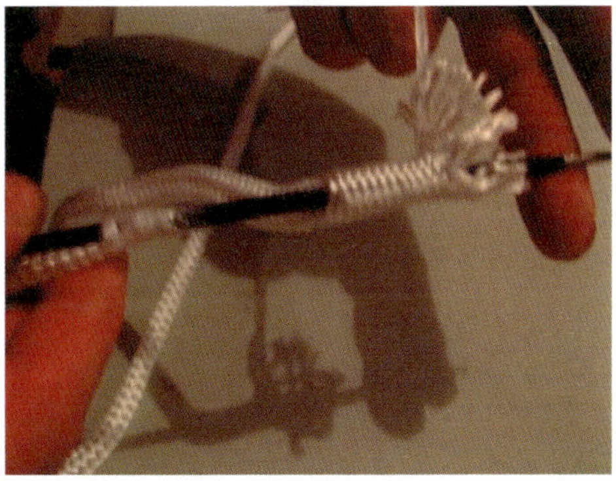

E

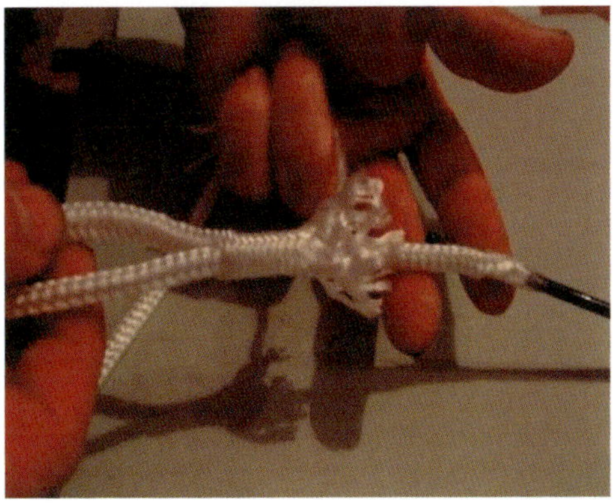

F

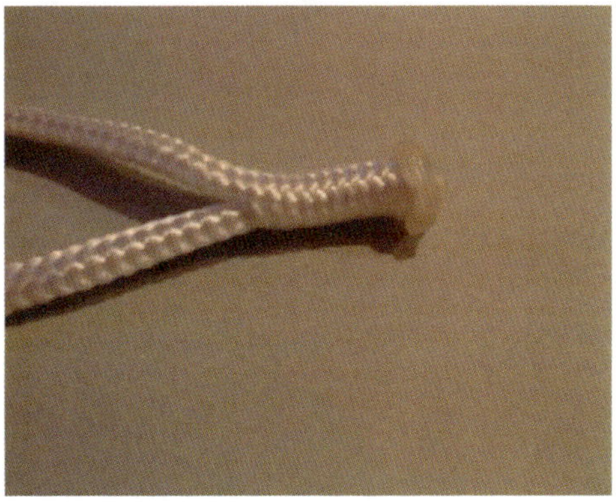

Congratulations you have now completed your rope halter!

For more information on trick and natural horse training

WWW.TRICKHORSEUK.COM

To discover the equestrian and wildlife art of Suzanne Fargher

WWW.SUZANNEFARGHER.COM

Made in the USA
Lexington, KY
06 February 2012